"A united and close family is one of my values, but I was having difficulties dealing with my kid's big feelings. I felt triggered by those situations, and it was difficult to feel close to him.

"Jen's work has completely changed this for me. Her tools have helped me to have a warm relationship with my kid where I don't need to be the boss anymore. My five-year-old has a rich vocabulary to express his feelings and needs, is willing to participate in problem-solving conversations, and many times, he is the one who finds the solution that works for both of us!

"Of course, there are still moments where we (both!) have big feelings, but we have a starting point of conversation where we listen and feel close to each other, and we really do feel as though we're on the same team."

—*Ana, Mexican parent of one living in the United States*

"The parenting information and tools that Jen teaches have prevented an untold amount of child-parent headbutting and made us do a 135-degree turn in how we thought we were going to raise our kiddos.

"Our goal now is to consciously parent, in a way that models our goals and values, by integrating every individual's feelings and needs, and now heads get butted far less often!"

—*Amanda and Benson, Chinese Canadian parents of two living in Canada*

"If you're like me, you've always wanted to make a difference in the world, to further social justice causes, but you then find yourself smack in the middle of parenthood, feeling too busy with the day-to-day concerns of parenting to honor your intentions. And that's what I love about Jen's approach! She helps me see how it is the very act of parenting in alignment with my values that enables me to disrupt patriarchy and racism. And with my tendency to be a worrier and overachiever, it helps me give myself credit for the important work I'm already doing through my commitment to a collaborative, nonpunitive approach to parenthood that meets both mine and my child's needs."

—*Jamie, Queer Latinx parent of one living in the United States*

"When I only had one young child, it seemed quite easy to parent in alignment with my values of respectful parenting. As my older son turned four, with the arrival of his brother, we started having lots of conflict. I realized I didn't know how to help our family function well and ended up using a lot of consequences, which only created more conflict!

"I've learned new tools from Jen to navigate everyday challenges that used to seem overwhelming, in a way that is aligned with my value of respect for all people. I'm also inspired by her vision that we can help change the world we live in by raising our children in a way that fosters respect and equity, and I'm glad that the tools that make my life easier now will have this wider positive impact as my children go out into the world knowing what it means to truly be in respectful relationships with others."

—*Genevieve, French Canadian parent of two living in Mexico*

"In becoming parents, we always said we didn't want to lose ourselves in favor of putting our child first all the time, but we also knew we didn't want the power-dynamic approach with our child that parents, and ourselves as teachers, so often fall into (or feel forced into).

"The Problem-Solving Approach that Jen has taught us has been exactly what we were looking for, helping to guide us in showing our child the respect they deserve, and enabling us to involve them as part of the decision-making process of our family. This means that we don't really have 'tantrums' (them *or* us)! As we try to consider everyone's needs, we're usually able to take an action that meets all of them. It's really hard to break out of the way we were socialized, but so incredibly worth it. We feel like we understand our child, that our child understands us, and through this work, we've also come to better understand ourselves and each other."

—*Emma and Alex, White British parents of one living in England*

"Just realizing that I have the tools and understanding of how to problem-solve in my family has been transformative. Not only am I now able to confidently begin to navigate the world of dealing with a headstrong but sensitive child, but I also know that I am basing it on ideas and values that resonate with our family. Having Jen's resources has empowered me to be a better parent and start laying the foundation for a strong relationship with my child and family for the future."

—*Yasmin, South African of Indian descent and parent of one*

"I'm very happy to have learned the Problem-Solving Approach. Just today I was in the usual tussle with my four-year-old over having a shower. I was about to override her resistance and spray water on her. I thought of what I'd learned from Jen and managed to pause for a moment. I tried a three-minute problem-solving conversation. This led to a quick game. She was then in and out of the shower within five minutes with no resistance at all. I highly recommend giving Jen's approach a try. By focusing on both of our needs, and setting fewer limits, I'm fighting less with my kid and slowly learning to appreciate her just as she is."

—*Thofique, Indian British parent of two living in Singapore*

"A year ago, I was scared. Scared of my young toddler's big feelings and how they made me feel, scared of becoming an embarrassingly permissive parent, scared of the resentment building in my marriage . . .

"Now I'm feeling more confident in my ability to identify and uphold boundaries rooted in our values, calmly support my child through age-appropriate meltdowns, approach disagreements with my spouse in a more collaborative way—and remain compassionate with myself when all of that falls apart."

—*Brittany, biracial African American parent of two living in Canada*

"Discovering this problem-solving-based approach has given our family clarity and is aligned with our value for collaboration. Knowing that we are going to work together to meet everyone's needs has resulted in less stress for everyone."

—*Miranda, First Nations parent of one living in Canada*

"Jen's work has given me a precious gift: a different attitude toward, *a different perspective of*, children. Just this morning, we were running late, and my daughter took off for a moment, and came back with my lipstick smeared all over her lips and interesting eye-pencil marks all over her face. Before I encountered Jen's approach, I would have scolded her, and been really irritated. I would have done this because my perspective, *my attitude*, toward children would have been: 'Children are generally mischievous and troublemakers. They need us adults to keep them in line.' And on the other side of that: 'Can't she see that we're already running late?' Instead, I took a breath, and then I laughed. This encouraged her to say: 'Mama, you left it on the bed!' And I said: 'Yes—I did,' and as we got her cleaned up, I thought: *Jen's approach has changed everything.*

"I see children differently. I see children as full and equal human beings, deserving of respect, deserving of dignity. I really see my daughter, and not just that: I see through her eyes. I see what it's like to be small, to not have 100 percent impulse control, to want to try out things, to be curious, to want to express oneself. In her world, time isn't what it is in my world. Jen's approach makes it possible for me to see life through the eyes of the child, and the result is that I am less stressed about the small daily things that children do (or don't do). I am less in 'lecture mode.' Our relationship is marked with more ease because, for the most part, I respond with an attitude of trust: 'she is not throwing a tantrum just to make trouble.' It could be that she's overwhelmed or tired. I approach the situation with curiosity, and when I can't figure something out by talking with her, I make a presumption from the perspective that accords my child the most respect."

—*Elizabeth, Kenyan parent of two*

PARENTING

HOW TO USE CONNECTION & COLLABORATION

BEYOND

TO TRANSFORM YOUR FAMILY—AND THE WORLD

POWER

JEN LUMANLAN, MS, MEd

SASQUATCH BOOKS
SEATTLE

SASQUATCH BOOKS with colophon is a registered trademark of Penguin Random House LLC

27 26 25 24 23   9 8 7 6 5 4 3 2 1

Editor: Hannah Elnan | Production editor: Isabella Hardie
Designer: Anna Goldstein | Typeface (headings): Carrie VTC by Tré Seals

Library of Congress Cataloging-in-Publication Data is available.

ISBN: 978-1-63217-448-2

Printed by employee-owned printer Friesens in Canada.

Sasquatch Books
1325 Fourth Avenue, Suite 1025
Seattle, WA 98101

SasquatchBooks.com

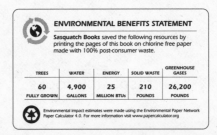

ENVIRONMENTAL BENEFITS STATEMENT

Sasquatch Books saved the following resources by printing the pages of this book on chlorine free paper made with 100% post-consumer waste.

TREES	WATER	ENERGY	SOLID WASTE	GREENHOUSE GASES
60	4,900	25	210	26,200
FULLY GROWN	GALLONS	MILLION BTUs	POUNDS	POUNDS

Environmental impact estimates were made using the Environmental Paper Network Paper Calculator 4.0. For more information visit www.papercalculator.org

For Carys,
who got me into this whole mess in the first place

What if I told you that your ideas about politics
are actually just your ideas about childhood extrapolated?

—*Dr. Toby Rollo*

LAND ACKNOWLEDGMENT

This book was drafted on the traditional lands of the Nimíipuu (Nez Perce) in what is now known as McCall, Idaho; edited on the traditional lands of the sqaǰət (Lower Skagit), swədəbš (Swinomish), suqʷabš (Suquamish), sduhubš (Snohomish), and dxʷlilap (Tulalip) tribes on what is now known as Whidbey Island, Washington; and finalized on the traditional lands of the Lisjan Ohlone in what is now known as Berkeley, California.

These groups are the rightful stewards of these lands, both in the past and present. While they can never be fully compensated for the harms that the legacy of colonialism has wrought, I pay the Shuumi Land Tax as recognition that more than words are needed, and I encourage others to engage meaningfully (including financially) with their local Indigenous communities.

If you are a resident of the East Bay (San Francisco Bay Area) and/or would like to support the Lisjan Ohlone, you can calculate and pay your Shuumi Land Tax at SogoreaTe-LandTrust.org /Shuumi-Land-Tax/. To find out which tribes were and are present in your local area, visit Native-Land.ca.

CONTENTS

PREFACE

For most of my life, I've been deeply impacted by the ideas in this book—the connections between our children's difficult behavior and the social problems we face—without really knowing anything about them. And unless your family was very radical, it's most likely that these have affected you as well.

I was born just northeast of London, England. My father grew up in a Yorkshire mining town where coal dust hung thick in the air—the mining unions were strong then and wouldn't be crushed by Prime Minister Maggie Thatcher until the 1980s—and my mother's father worked his way up from a similar background to being an upper-middle-class corporate executive. Her parents disapproved of the match, and I remember the delicious thrill of figuring out that their wedding anniversary fell the day after her eighteenth birthday, when they no longer needed her parents' permission—although my dad recently told me my childhood math was mistaken, and they waited longer out of respect for her parents. My mum very much looked forward to having children, but she really wanted a baby who would need her—and unfortunately, I didn't fit the bill. I had a self-sufficient personality from the very beginning, and she didn't really know how to be in a relationship with me. I'm told that at eight months old I would sit quietly in my crib after waking up, paging through picture books. My dad would come home from work to find my mum playing with my baby sister, and me in a corner by myself, wrapped up in my own world.

Looking back, I see echoes of the pressures that capitalism, patriarchy, and even White supremacy put on our family. We were shielded from the effects of capitalism a little by the English welfare state; for a time, we lived in council-owned housing (reserved for low-income families) while my dad spent the weekends building a house in rural eastern England where land was cheap. He was a woodworking teacher during the week—I picked up my confidence to tackle pretty major home-improvement projects from him!—and he signed up for night classes and took on extra responsibilities as a deputy headmaster so we could be more secure. Yet financial concerns were ever-present: one day when I was cold in my bedroom, I turned the radiator up from its usual setting of two to its maximum of six. Radiators take a long time to warm up, and later that evening, as my mum dried me off after my bath with our scratchy old towels, we both suddenly realized the room was *very hot*. I wasn't punished, but I still remember the shame I felt as I stepped slowly down the stairs to confess my sin to my dad. The message was clearly received: *we do not waste.*

While there were moments of closeness—I remember regular hugs with my mum after evening baths—our family had a highly patriarchal structure. My sister and I were permitted a good deal of freedom in how we spent our time, mostly climbing trees and creating games in the garden, but it was crystal clear who held the power and what behavior was expected of us. We were to say "please" and "thank you" and finish everything on our plates or there wouldn't be any pudding (the British term for "dessert"). When I was "lazy" in my pronunciation of a word, which made me sound like a working-class person, my mum would make me say it "correctly" ten times in a row—a humiliation that stings to remember today as much as it did when I was eight. Deference to authority, and understanding how to deliver what authorities wanted to see, were prized, which prepared me to do well in school—but not to think for myself. Patriarchal systems rely on people—especially working-class people—knowing their place, and parents are the agents of that socialization.

I didn't need to acknowledge White supremacy (the belief that the White race is inherently superior to other races and that White people should have control over people of other races) when I was young because everyone around me was White. There were no Black, Indigenous, and People of Color (BIPOC) children in my primary school (70 children) or village (population 500), and there were only two in my high school (750 children). I was in the same form (homeroom) as a girl from Mauritius; her parents owned a retirement home (which marked her as "weird"), and she was one of the smartest people in a school where putting in the minimum effort was the name of the game. Several times, a boy in our form made racist comments toward her; I remember giving him a dirty look and turning back toward the girl, who was my friend, knowing in my head and in my gut that something bad had just happened, but each time feeling completely blindsided and not knowing how to speak up even if I'd thought of doing it. My White privilege shielded me from seeing the need to engage more forcefully on her behalf—by telling him to stop or by reporting his comments to a teacher. I knew that what he had said was wrong, but I didn't see that I had any responsibility to put it right.

Aside from the glory of the European explorers who "discovered" far-flung corners of the world, we didn't learn about history before the First World War or outside of Europe—in school the running joke was that "there wasn't enough of it"—so I was conveniently ignorant of England's colonial history, the country's role in the slave trade, and even the cultures of recent immigrants who were present in more urban parts of England.

One day when I was ten, the kids who went home to eat lunch came back to report that there was an ambulance parked outside my family's house. My sister and I assumed it was for the old man who lived across the street—until the end of the day when we were each summoned to the headmaster's office—an unusual occurrence for a Good Girl like me. I remember the cold metal of the headmaster's desk pressing against my bare legs. With an arm around each of us, my dad told my sister and me that the postman had found our mum collapsed outside while washing windows. As my dad and sister cried together, I wondered why I felt so neutral. Dazed, rather than devastated. The coroner's report said that she had died of a ruptured splenic artery; I didn't learn until years later that this had been caused by anorexia nervosa, and many more years passed before I realized that this can be a way for women to manipulate their bodies for the approval of the male gaze.

While this was obviously a difficult time in my life, it didn't affect me as deeply as it would have if I'd had a good relationship with my mum—and there were certainly lessons learned in that period about stuffing down feelings. I remember passing my dad's room and seeing him cradling my mum's jewelry box, crying—after a long second of indecision I sneaked silently down the stairs on tiptoe, knowing he wouldn't want me to see, since expressions of weakness by male authority figures are seen as unacceptable in patriarchal systems. My dad didn't need to tell me this; I had already internalized this idea without being told.

The most obvious way that White supremacy showed up in my family of origin was in its power structure and in how conflict was handled. (White supremacy doesn't always take the shape of racism. Back in 1999, Tema Okun described how she and others see it show up in organizations in the form of ideas like perfectionism, a sense of urgency, defensiveness, there only being one right way, paternalism, either/or thinking, power hoarding, fear of open conflict, and individualism.) Not long after my mum died, my dad and I disagreed about something at the dinner table. I don't remember what it was, but I was pretty sure I was right and he'd misunderstood or didn't know what I knew and was refusing to consider my perspective. I felt consumed by anger in a way that I don't think I had experienced before and got up to leave the table, but the back legs of the chair caught on the shag rug and it tipped over. I ran up to my room, and he shouted, *"Get back down here!"* in such a thunderous voice that I was terrified, even though he had never physically hurt me. I wanted to stay in my room, but I didn't dare; the threat of what might happen in response to further resistance was unknowably worse than what would happen if I complied. Wishing I could be smaller, so small he couldn't see me, I crept back down (funny how many pivotal moments happened on those stairs, that place of transition. . .), picked up the chair, and sat on it. My dad said, in a voice trembling with barely controlled fury: "You would never have *dared* to do that if your mum were here." I don't think I was punished, but I understood that if there was a difference of opinion, only one person's idea would be accepted as valid, and it wouldn't be mine. I was not permitted to show frustration or anger. I was to preserve a sense of harmony at the expense of understanding my needs, expressing them, and working to meet them alongside the needs of others.

Throughout my teenage years I repressed my feelings and ideas, as I was afraid of creating conflict. There was a period of time when my father would lecture me every night as if I were his student over a perceived shortcoming of mine, and I would stand mutely, knees aching from being locked for so long and brain shut down beyond the basic functioning needed to mumble "yes" and "no" at regular intervals, until he had argued himself out. I only recently realized this is the cause of one of my biggest triggers—being interrupted by my husband—while interviewing an expert on intergenerational trauma for my podcast. Because I wasn't strong enough to resist outwardly (through behavior that would be labeled "defiant"), I turned inward and exerted control over what I ate—"resisting" patriarchal control but still playing into both patriarchal and White-supremacy-based ideas of the ideal female body shape.

Perhaps it might not be enormously surprising that, at age nineteen, I married a narcissist with a drug problem whom I met while traveling in the United States. We were the perfect match: I was desperate to feel wanted and needed, and he knew exactly how to push me to the edge of despair and then reel me back in with "love." One time, I drove for two days to rescue him after a drug binge— veering in at every rest stop in the western half of Montana for the contents of my innards to explode out—to find he had pawned his wedding ring to pay for drugs.

He told me he felt most loved by me when I came to get him after these binges, so I kept coming.

Recovery from that relationship, which the U.S. Immigration and Customs Enforcement deemed emotionally abusive, was long and slow—and done without therapy, due to my lack of health insurance. It took me a long time to fully trust my current husband, Alvin. For the first couple of years after we lived together, I would freak out if he left the house in the morning while I was still asleep. I would call him in a panic to find out if he was on a drug binge when actually, of course, he was just at work. Even though ours is a marriage of more-or-less equals, I still see the effects of White supremacy, patriarchy, and capitalism in our relationship. He assumed I would take his name when we got married, and was not interested in any discussion of a different plan. Once again I was angry but still had no idea how to navigate conflict in a healthy way, so I simply submitted to his wish rather than risking the wedding over a name. I used to try to protect his feelings when our daughter was dysregulated or "misbehaving" by managing her so he wasn't inconvenienced, although now he is making a conscious effort to regulate *himself* in difficult moments and understand her needs.

When our daughter started day care, it was assumed that I would manage her drop-offs and pickups, lunches, keeping extra clothes at school, and interactions with the teachers—on top of the routine checkups and sickness appointments at the doctor's office and running our home. I had a job that paid well but that I didn't really enjoy while trying to build a business so we could pay our mortgage; we were recipients of a first-time homeowner's loan that is often unavailable to Black families. When people asked how I was doing, I would give the expected answer: the sigh, the eyebrow raise, the wry smile, and the typical: "Oh, busy."

For a long time, I didn't see the connections between things that were happening in my home and broader cultural forces. I went back to school for a master's degree in psychology that focused on child development, and another in education, both of which confirmed the narrative I'd learned: "success" means doing well in school, going to college, gaining authority through credentials, getting a job, and not being a burden on the state. I started the *Your Parenting Mojo* podcast to share with other parents what I was learning about the scientific research on parenting and child development, and then developed a Parenting Membership to help those who needed more support in applying the ideas they were hearing on the show.

Over time, I noticed two parallel trends. I was working with parents who had a lot of questions about their children's behavior that mostly boiled down to: "How do I get my child to . . . ?"

And at the same time, the parents asking these questions were *hurting*. They were exhausted from working multiple jobs or spending twenty-four seven with their children or running from one after-school activity to the next to try to give their child the best start. They were at the end of their rope because their child resisted them every step of the way: throwing tantrums, stalling, talking back, being defiant. And they felt completely isolated because they didn't have a "village" or even a relationship with their family members where they could discuss anything meaningful.

Eventually I saw the connection between these ideas: these parents were exhausted because they were swimming in the White supremacist, patriarchal, capitalist-based view of scarcity where individuals have to earn the right to live. They had to get their child to outwardly conform to the social norms of these systems, which give their children access to resources. To accomplish this, the child had to learn how to follow orders from authority figures—which was the very same way that their parents had raised them—so their child was fighting back, kicking and screaming. The power structures out in the world were being replicated in their own homes. You can't have power over someone without hurting them, even if it's unintentionally.

And these parents were affected by the pain caused by their own parents having said (verbally or nonverbally): "I don't care about your needs. You must learn to disregard your needs so I can be comfortable, and because I want what's best for you, and because you won't be successful in the world if you make your needs known."

Most of our parents:

- Wanted us to be perfect, and to do things by ourselves without help.

- Saw both us and our behavior as either good or bad, right or wrong.

- Used their power to keep us in our place and didn't allow direct conflict.

- Made decisions for us without understanding our perspective.

- Protected certain family members' feelings at the expense of everyone else's needs.

- Focused on individual roles and keeping people in their place.

- Required linear, logical thinking and ignored emotional and physical intelligence.

- Held a scarcity mentality: there was never enough money or resources, and we had to get our share.

- Focused on getting tasks done above valuing relationships.

- Hoarded power and shamed those with differing opinions.

- Celebrated financial and intellectual successes (and skills that could contribute to those) above all other achievements.

- Owned more, bigger, and better resources individually rather than communally (house, car, pool, lawn mower, etc.).

- Paid for services to replace relationships of care.

The societal forces of White supremacy, patriarchy, and capitalism weren't just happening "out there" in the world; they were present in our homes while we were growing up. They hurt us then by creating a separation between us and our parents or caregivers, and they're still hurting us now. They caused us to think there was something wrong with us for having feelings that others found threatening, for wanting to be seen and understood in our full humanity, and for caring about things other than money. Because we grew up steeped in these ideas, the easiest thing to do is simply to replicate this environment with our own children. And if we don't make a choice to do things differently, we'll end up hurting our children in the very same way that we were hurt.

But what if we could see our children, know them, and respect them for who they truly are? What if we learned how to meet our real needs—*not* what society tells us we should want—as well as our children's needs? Then our children wouldn't act out, because acting out is the best way a child knows how to say: "My needs aren't being met." When their needs are met, they stop acting out. They will know that we see them and respect them, and they will see and respect us too.

Having learned respect from us, they will treat others with respect and ask to be treated with respect. When they learn boundaries from us, they won't get walked all over by others (or dragged into situations they know aren't safe), and will respect the boundaries that others set. When we share power with our children at home, they know how to (and are willing to!) share power with others. In so doing, they will take this model out into the wider world.

This is how change happens: one drop rippling outward.

My own daughter doesn't "act out," and because we've been using the tools in this book for a while, she's even able to point out when I fall into old habits. A couple of years ago, I was feeling stressed because I was preparing slides for a workshop I was delivering the next day. I came out of the room where I was working to make a snack of stewed apples, and my then five-year-old daughter Carys (rhymes with "Paris") asked if I could put frozen blueberries in with them.

Me: "No!"

Carys: "Why not?"

Me: "Because I've already put the cinnamon in, and I think blueberries and cinnamon will taste terrible together."

Carys: "Well, can you pull out a portion for me so I can put blueberries in mine?"

Me: "Oh. Yes. Of course. I thought you were saying you wanted them to be *cooked* together."

Carys: "See! We found a way that meets both of our needs."

Even when I wasn't using the very tools I teach, they've become so ingrained in our relationship that she can remind me when I forget. And this serves us in any disagreement we have, from toothbrushing to screen time to sugar consumption to bedtime to not wanting to get dressed in the morning. She knows I will treat her needs with the same level of respect as I treat my own, and that I will try to meet both of our needs if at all possible. This reduces the amount of time we spend in conflict and creates time for us to interact in more loving, deeply connected ways.

And the respect moves outward from there.

If men truly respected women, women would be safe (and seen, and "feminine" qualities wouldn't be a bad thing).

If White people truly respected Black, Indigenous, and People of Color (BIPOC), they would be safe (and Blackness and Indigenousness would be valued by people of all races).

If we respected the earth, we would find ways to meet all of our needs while living within the earth's capacity.

So while it may have seemed like our politically liberal ideas on topics like White supremacy, patriarchy, and capitalism were completely unrelated to the struggles we've been having with our child's behavior, it turns out that they are intimately connected. The way we treat our children shapes how they will treat others, which means that the changes we want to see in our world start at home. This book will show you how to do it—and, at the same time, will actually make parenting easier for you.

AUTHOR'S NOTE

WHO THIS BOOK IS FOR

This was one of the hardest sections of the book to write because I wanted to make sure the book includes everyone who wants to be included while also acknowledging the privileges I hold.

Starting with me: I'm a White, cisgender, heterosexual, married, able-bodied, partnered (which means I get breaks from parenting!) woman, and I'm raising a biracial child who presents closely enough to White that she will gain many of the advantages of White privilege.

I have a complicated relationship with money. My parents didn't have a lot of it; I have an old recipe book of my mum's where she budgeted for groceries to the penny, and a letter from her to her sister dated eight months before I was born (did she know she was pregnant?) saying that she and my dad were trying to save enough money to visit her sister two hundred miles away in three months' time but weren't sure if they'd be able to afford it. I don't think that any adult in the generations before mine had a bachelor's degree. Not having money is a narrative that is baked into who I am, even when my husband and I were earning enough to put us well inside the top 5 percent of earners. At the time of writing, we are much closer to the US median, and money is a stressor once again. A structure in our garden is leaking rainwater onto electrical wiring, a new crack has appeared in a retaining wall that will probably fail in next winter's rains, and we don't have the money to fix either of them. But I do "own" (i.e., pay the mortgage on) a nice but not ostentatious house in the San Francisco Bay Area at a monthly rate that is now lower than the going rental rate for a two-bedroom apartment. I had the privilege to not be redlined out of a neighborhood or a home loan, and I know that if things ever got really bad, I could access more funding through formal (e.g., banks) and informal (e.g., friends and family) channels.

This book is especially for White parents ... but not just for White parents

White people have spent generations telling parents of other races, and especially Black and Indigenous parents, that our way of parenting is best, and if they could *just do things like we do them*, their children would be successful too (in a White-supremacist, patriarchal, capitalist world). This approach pervades:

- Government policy (including forced separations of Indigenous families, government-sanctioned breakups of families through the mechanism of slavery, and the overrepresentation of Indigenous and Black children in foster care compared with White children).

- Academic research (which talks about closing "gaps" between the success of Indigenous/Black children and White children using interventions like grit and a growth mindset, rather than by eliminating poverty).

- Parenting advice (which assumes all parents want the same things for their child as a privileged White person does).

As a White parent, it isn't my place to tell parents who don't identify as White how to raise children. I fully recognize that many parents who don't identify as White make choices that are designed to help their children succeed in a White supremacist world. The focus of this book is on understanding and meeting parents' and children's needs, and BIPOC parents may be forced to do things like get their child to wear certain clothes and shoes, arrange their hair in ways the child might not choose, and go to bed early so they don't seem sleepy in school, because a White parent or teacher might call Child Protective Services if their child seems "unkempt" or unable to fully participate at school. Black parents have also told me that they feel pressure to make their child "behave," because a misbehaving Black child is judged as representing all children of their racial group, rather than being seen as an individual, and may be perceived by White people as "dangerous."

My daughter went through a phase in preschool where she only wanted to wear fleecy clothes, which meant wearing pajamas to school. I was *never once* afraid that the teachers would think I was an unfit parent. When I dosed her with pain medicine that I hadn't yet paid for during a full-on ear infection–induced meltdown in a drug store as a toddler, I had *zero fear* for my or her safety. That BIPOC parents must decide to keep their child safe from White parents and teachers rather than meeting their child's other needs is a massive failure on my part and on the part of all White people. If using the strategies in this book could put your child's safety in danger, or if they don't fit with your cultural practices, *please don't use them.*

There are even people who say that a White person shouldn't write this book, because we should take the lead from BIPOC authors. I agree; we absolutely must read what BIPOC people have to say about these issues and learn from them first. I reference many books by BIPOC authors throughout this book, and more are listed in the Resources section on page 201. I also hear repeatedly from BIPOC authors that White people need to do our own work, and I haven't been able to find a book by a BIPOC author that explicitly tells White parents how to work to overcome White supremacy, patriarchy, and capitalism *through the daily interactions we have with our children that may on the surface seem like they're about discipline.*

Of course, we need to read children's books with BIPOC protagonists, and talk with our children about these topics. But we know that our children do what we *do* rather than what we *say.* We can tell them not to swear, but if we swear when we're around them, they're probably going to end up swearing. We can tell them: "Respect BIPOC people. Respect women. Respect the earth." But if our daily actions with them communicate, "I have more power than you, and I'm going to use it to make you comply with my wishes," then they're going to end up using their own power against others in harmful ways. I hope that, through this book, I will both amplify the voices of BIPOC people and also reduce the need for them to expend their precious time, energy, and resources educating White and relatively privileged people about how to break down the White supremacist, patriarchal, capitalist structures that hurt everyone, but hurt BIPOC people most of all.

Even though we see the effects of these social forces most clearly in Eurocentric countries, they can be seen wherever White colonization, European religions, and capitalism are practiced—and the degree of the effects is usually aligned with the degree of practice. When I asked a racially diverse group of parents to whom I should address the book, one of them wrote, and several agreed, that: "I don't think the book will help White people more than People of Color. I honestly believe that anyone who reads it will benefit from it regardless of our race; we are all partaking in White supremacy, whether we are aware of it or not . . ." So while White parents have the most work to do here, this book is for anyone who lives in a culture where White supremacy, patriarchy, and capitalism have extensively shaped us and our interactions with each other; who realizes that they may have been complicit in upholding these values in their family; and who wants to take steps to change this.

This book is especially for privileged parents . . . but not just for privileged parents

All of the parents whose stories are featured in this book do come from *relative* financial privilege. They all have enough time to listen to my podcast (which is how I met them) and a warm place to sleep, and they know where their next meal is coming from. I offer sliding-scale pricing for access to my paid courses and memberships; some of them pay the highest rate, while others are paying the lowest published rate or even a special "nobody turned away" price. All of them can afford to spend at least a few dollars and/or a few hours a month learning about parenting.

But in many ways, these parents are not privileged at all. Some were raised on welfare by single parents. Some are single parenting now because they have experienced abuse by their former partner. Several were physically or emotionally abused as children, and a good number of them are recovering from drug and alcohol addictions, which, at their root, were caused by their pain of not fitting in (to a White supremacist, patriarchal, capitalist culture and a family that was trying to train them to function in that culture). Many feel triggered when their child's behavior reminds them of this old trauma, which brings it back to the surface.

I sometimes hear parents who are having a hard time say: "These respectful parenting methods sound great if you don't have three jobs and a limited supply of patience. I don't have time to sit next to my child and empathize every time they're having a tantrum after school. I have to get to work." The key here is to recognize that, in using these methods, *you won't have to sit next to your child every day after school, because they won't have tantrums every day after school when you can understand and address their needs.* Obviously, I can't guarantee your child will never have a tantrum again. But if you are trying to meet their needs if at all possible most of the time, you will find that your relationship with your child gets easier and more harmonious because you will have addressed the root cause of these recurring patterns of behavior. This approach *gives* you time and energy and patience with just a little investment on the front end.

This book is mostly for parents with children under the age of ten (but the tools "work" with people of all ages)

Readers usually want the examples in a book to be relevant to their situation, so readers with children aged one to ten will be most at home here. Ultimately these tools are applicable to all people in any relationship, and many parents I work with are surprised to find that applying them in relationships with their spouses, parents, and colleagues is just as useful and rewarding as working with their child.

You can download free resources to help you use the tools in this book—including full-page, printable versions of the diagrams and templates, as well as how-to videos and a book summary to share with family members. Please visit https://www.YourParentingMojo. com/BookBonuses.

Whatever your identity and degree of privilege, I hope you find the Problem-Solving Approach I describe in the book to be useful. I'm rooting for you and your child, and for *all* children everywhere.

TERMINOLOGY

I have tried to be very intentional about the terminology I use in the book, and I'd like to make sure we're on the same page about a few things before we start. Please note that acceptable terminology on these issues does change over time and may be outdated by the time you read the book.

- I know that not all people who provide care to children are parents, but for the sake of brevity, I refer to "parents" rather than "parents/caregivers."

- All of the tools I describe can be used by parents of any gender, so I use "parent" rather than "Mom" or "Dad," except when I'm specifically describing the experiences of parents identifying as moms or dads.

- "Cisgender" refers to someone whose gender identity matches the sex they were assigned at birth, although we should acknowledge that genitalia are ambiguous more often than we might think! I am a cisgender woman: I identify as female, and I have female genitalia and XX chromosomes (which is not a 100 percent reliable indicator, but the closest we have).

- In keeping with the results of a panel I convened to develop antiracist policies for my business, I have made a stylistic decision to capitalize both "Black" and "White" in this book. Many style guides now capitalize "Black" to confer a sense of power and respect to Black people. In acknowledgment that both Black and White are social constructs (and also to avoid lowercase "white" being seen as normal, while uppercase "Black" is other-than-normal), I capitalize both when referring to race.

- I use the term "BIPOC (Black, Indigenous, and People of Color)" because it is a commonly understood acronym that seems to be preferred by the people to whom it refers.

- I use the term "Eurocentric countries" to refer to countries where people of White European origin predominantly hold the positions of power (e.g., Europe, North America, Australia, and New Zealand).

- Rather than arbitrarily switching back and forth between the non-inclusive "he" and "she" to refer to a child's gender, I use the gender-neutral term "they," except when describing fictional situations with more than one child where genders are introduced to make the anecdotes easier to follow.

Many of the ideas in the book are supported by academic research. Wherever possible, I've included endnotes to podcast episodes that I've produced in support of specific points. Each episode is an interview with an expert or my synthesis of the related research and contains more detail and peer-reviewed references to support the ideas in this book. To avoid cluttering the text with numbers, endnotes are organized by chapter and page numbers in the Notes section (see page 212).

LETTING GO OF WHAT YOU KNOW

It's no secret that parenting in our culture is really freaking hard, but not for the reasons you think. It's not hard because of anything your child—or you—is doing wrong. You may wonder how on earth *this* book could be any more helpful than all the other books you've already read, podcasts you've listened to, and ideas you've implemented. After all, the sticker and star charts, counting to three, consequences, time-outs, 'catching' them being good, praise, setting expectations, and giving choices were all supposed to 'work', but they haven't.

On a daily basis, your child doesn't listen. They ignore you; they "don't hear you," even when you call them twenty times; they stall; they resist; they look you right in the eye and do the exact thing you just asked them not to do. And then they refuse to do the things you ask them to do.

You may be struggling to keep your cool through all of this. Perhaps days begin somewhat smoothly . . . but then come the demands:

"I want the *green* spoon, not the red one."

"I don't *like* these crackers today."

"So-and-so is *looking at me!*"

You accommodate these requests for as long as you can; after all, you love your children, right? But eventually it gets to be too much: you feel walked all over, taken advantage of, and just plain resentful. Once meals are prepared, cleaning is sort of done, and the laundry mountain is at least reduced in volume, there may not be any time left for you to do the things you love. Or move your body in ways that feel good. Or sleep.

Conventional parenting advice is pretty clear on what your job is here: it's to get your child to do what you tell them to do. When your child does what you ask without complaining; doesn't do what you tell them not to do (also without complaining); plays nicely with their siblings or peers; and fulfills teachers' expectations at school, then you are a Good Parent. And then you can relax, and maybe take some time for yourself. Even many so-called respectful parenting approaches argue that it's the parent's job to be in charge and obtain their child's compliance—insisting that your way is the right way because young children are not equipped to handle the power of understanding and meeting people's needs.

Whether we were Good Parented as children, or whether our parents struggled with their own issues while we basically raised ourselves, we probably learned to toe the line, play nicely with others, and do well (or well enough) in school. And either way, the end result was the same: we learned that our needs were not as important as theirs, that we would only be welcomed into the family when our behavior met certain expectations, and that deviating from those expectations would cause rejection and the withdrawal of love and approval.

It may seem as though we "turned out fine." Or perhaps that's just the version of us we like to show the world, and underneath, things are not fine at all. We may feel afraid to show parts of ourselves that still seem unacceptable and unlovable—to the wider world, to our extended family and friends, even to our partner. It may seem like we're a fraud, looking like we're keeping it together in work, parenting, and mental stability—and if we can just keep up the façade, nobody will find out. We may feel disconnected from our own children, since we spend most of our time telling them to do things and not to do other things and keeping them from trying to kill each other.

This is just what parenting is like, right?

PARENTING WITH POWER AND CONTROL

Parent Maria grew up in a very religious Australian family where God and Maria's dad were in charge. The approach of counting to three and requiring obedience on the third count was popular when Maria was young, but in Maria's house, her parents would count to *one*, at which time the children would have to agree to whatever was being asked and do it "with a good attitude." With eight siblings younger than her, Maria's role in the family was to keep the peace, making sure nobody upset her parents, who were struggling with their own mental health challenges. Any attempt to assert her own ideas about her body, her decisions, or her life was met with consequences, punishment, and shame.

Years later, when Maria's oldest daughter Isabel was six weeks old, she was already asserting her strong will: she always wanted to be held in an upright position and would cry if her parents held her any other way. One day when Isabel was two, Maria made a plan to take her to the bakery up the road and have a doughnut together. In Maria's mind, it was going to be a beautiful, connecting experience, and all Isabel had to do was put her shoes on (experienced parents can already see where this is going, right?). Isabel lived by the motto: "don't do anything for yourself that you can get somebody else to do for you." Now that Isabel is eight, Maria can look at that attitude and see the amazing leadership skills of a CEO or a world-changing visionary, but sitting in front of her hall closet that day, Maria was The Boss, and those shoes were going to get on those feet, and Maria was not going to be the one who put them there. Cajolements followed; bribery followed; forty minutes later, the shoes were still not occupied.

They never made it to the bakery that day. But Maria didn't give in! She made sure that Isabel knew who was In Charge. And then Maria realized that she was essentially using the same tools that her parents had used, and that she might be able to reward and punish Isabel into cooperation now but this decision would come back to haunt their family later on. She didn't want to break Isabel's spirit. She really didn't want Isabel to follow in her own footsteps and become a people pleaser who would do whatever she was told as a young child and then rebel in her teenage years (as Maria had done). So Maria stopped using time-outs and "power-over" tools and tried to work with her daughter's spirited personality, although it was often still difficult.

For several years, Maria coped with these challenges, added a second strong-willed daughter, and figured she could slot in a third child. When her son was born just as spirited as the first two, though, all of a sudden she was right back where she started: constantly in a state of heightened arousal waiting for the next explosion of big feelings to happen, and fawning over her children whenever they cried to placate them back to calm and quiet, which was the only state that felt safe to her.

PARENTING BEYOND POWER—FROM FEAR TO JOY

I first met Maria when she joined my Taming Your Triggers course. When she introduced herself in the community, it was clear that she had a good deal of awareness about her struggles but didn't know how to cope when all three children were screaming at her at the same time. Using the exact tools that you're going to learn in this book, Maria realized that she is not responsible for other people's feelings, that she can identify her needs and make requests to get them met, and meet her family members' needs as well.

Her relationship with Isabel has *utterly* changed. A few years ago, their morning conversations would go like this:

Maria: "Get dressed."

Isabel: "No."

Maria: "Get dressed."

Isabel: "No."

After we started working together, Maria sat down next to Isabel one morning and gently asked: "What's going on for you? Why don't you want to get dressed?" Isabel replied: "I like knowing you're the last person who touches my clothes." Where Maria had previously seen resistance and defiance, now she saw a heart-melting need for connection—which she was absolutely willing to meet. Isabel would put on her own pants, and Maria snuggled with Isabel's top before helping to put that on, and then getting dressed each morning was no longer a struggle.

Maria had always worried about whether Isabel would be empathetic toward others: Maria once fell and sprained her ankle in front of seven-year-old Isabel—who just stepped over her and asked what they were going to have for morning snack. Maria has consistently modeled observing her children's behavior and saying things like: "Your sibling looks like they aren't really enjoying this at the moment; is that right?" Recently the family was sitting around the dinner table and the other children were teasing Maria when Isabel stepped in: "Mum's had a bit of a hard day today; I think she probably isn't up for being teased." Maria realized that all the acceptance of feelings and modeling of empathy and truly trying to understand her daughter's needs was paying off.

When asked to help, Isabel would previously have given her standard response: "No, I'm not doing that." Now when the family is getting ready to welcome guests for lunch, Isabel can see Maria's needs (order in the house, and collaboration with Isabel), articulate her own needs (warmth and comfort), and propose a solution that works for both of them ("It's too cold for me to clean up outside; is there something I can do inside?"), and Maria gladly accepts the help. She's doing two things through these interactions: enhancing the connection between them—and making life so much easier.

Maria is also starting to see how this approach is rippling out both in her family and into the wider world. Isabel was part of a group of "cool kids" at school that started bullying a child who was diagnosed with attention deficit hyperactivity disorder (ADHD). She disconnected from the group and decided to make friends with the child who had been bullied. Isabel still pushes back on authority when she feels it's warranted, like when a church group leader tries to get her to apologize to a sibling, and she responds: "That's not how it works in our family," then follows up later with a genuine apology when she's ready.

Maria is the first to admit that she is *not* a perfect parent—in fact, she said she felt like a fraud when I asked if I could share her story as an example of someone who is "doing it well." She's still working through her childhood trauma in therapy and messes things up on a regular basis (as we all do!). But she sees that if you use these methods *not perfectly but consistently,* the path gets smoother, easier, and more rewarding within her immediate family—and radiates from there out into the world.

WHY READ THIS BOOK?

The methods you're going to learn in this book will help you do three things:

1 **Heal yourself**

The majority of parents I work with set limits on their children's behavior when they already feel so walked all over that the child's last request becomes the straw that breaks the camel's back. They have no idea that they have needs themselves, never mind how to identify them or articulate a request to get them met, or how to set boundaries and limits when these are the most appropriate tools for the situation (so they aren't being walked all over until they explode on a regular basis). You'll learn how to understand your needs and make requests of others to help you meet them so you'll feel more relaxed and able to enjoy life—and your children!

2 **Create real connection with your child**

These tools will help you to raise a child in a relationship where you both truly respect each other's needs and can meet all of these needs the majority of the time. When your child can identify their needs and multiple strategies to meet these instead of getting attached to one single strategy, their needs can be met far more often. Your child will feel "seen" by you and will know that they are loved exactly as they are—which means they stop resisting you every step of the way, and start collaborating.

3 **Live your social justice values**

When we raise our children in a way that understands and respects their needs *and* our needs, they have a model for how they want to be treated in relationships and know how to set boundaries, instead of doing things that peers and authority figures tell them to do that goes against their values. They also go out into the world knowing how to understand other people's needs and hold these with just as much reverence as their own—and when more people can do that, we'll be better equipped to address social challenges like White supremacy, patriarchy, and capitalism.

HOW THIS BOOK IS STRUCTURED

In Chapter 1, I'll show how social forces like White supremacy, patriarchy, and capitalism have impacted us in our families, and how we will continue this cycle of trauma with our own children unless we choose to do something differently. If you're at the end of your rope with your child's behavior and prefer to dive into the tools that can make your life easier *right now*, then feel free to begin at Chapter 2 and circle back to Chapter 1 later.

Chapter 2 and the rest of the book dive deeply into reasons to move beyond traditional command-and-control parenting approaches like time-outs, punishments, and rewards, and provide guidance on how to use the Problem-Solving Approach so you can meet *your* needs as well as *your child's* needs. This will dramatically reduce the incidence of tantrums, meltdowns, resistance, and acting out from your child—because when your child's needs are met, they don't push back on you. It will also help you to find the peace and ease and joy in parenting that you're craving and that may seem so out of reach right now.

Throughout the book, you'll find a series of exercises to help you see how the concepts apply in your own life. Your brain processes information differently when you handwrite than when you type, so I encourage you to write your answers in a journal or on paper if you can. Set a timer for five minutes for each exercise and start writing without thinking too much. If you run out of things to write, start again from the beginning and see what else comes out the second time.

Most of all, this book is an invitation to begin a journey. I don't have *all* the answers; nobody does. I still mess up, and I certainly haven't "solved" these social challenges. But I also see how social movements start: with people trying something new, failing, trying again, and moving toward living in a way that is richly resonant with their values. Like Maria, the parents you'll meet in this book are already on this journey; they now find parenting less stressful than they ever imagined possible, and they see the ripples starting to touch the wider world. Will you join us?

CHAPTER 1:

SOCIETAL FORCES SHAPE OUR FAMILY LIFE

*How White Supremacy, Patriarchy, and Capitalism
Affect Our Relationships with Our Children*

Many of the challenges we have in our own lives originated from our needs being ignored or trampled when we were children, and when we do the same with our own children's needs, we're setting them up to struggle in the same ways we have struggled. These within-family difficulties echo the power structures of our broader culture. We will begin this chapter with a primer on the three main forces that underlie power structures in Eurocentric countries: White supremacy, patriarchy, and capitalism. Then we'll look at how they intertwine to affect us and our families.

WHITE SUPREMACY DIVIDES US

White supremacy is the idea that White people are superior to everyone else, and racism is one way we express that. But just as important as the Ku Klux Klan kind of overt racism are the ways that everyday parents like you and me, who might think of ourselves as "not racist," uphold White supremacist systems.

The concept of White supremacy has existed for at least as long as the concept of colonialism, as European colonizers took their (our) ways out into the world to "civilize" the "backward" natives. When they landed in what is now called the United States, colonizers were outnumbered by Indigenous people whose land they were stealing and, later, by the Africans whom they enslaved. The settlers created the category of Whiteness to put themselves above Indigenous and enslaved people, and to protect their financial assets. The idea that Whiteness holds value has been exported along with colonization and now permeates many cultures. White supremacy harms everyone because everyone suffers when we are divided from others and not allowed to live and express our full humanity. But BIPOC people are harmed most by White supremacy, which is why it's White people's responsibility to dismantle White supremacy as BIPOC people live and express *their* full humanity.

So Whiteness divides us by race, but it also divides us in lots of other ways: it creates winners (and losers); it divides nonconforming people from people who comply with societal norms (by doing things like dressing "appropriately," having the right amount of body hair in the right places, and behaving "correctly"); and it divides many of us from our neighbors and communities by making us feel like we have to do everything ourselves. It even creates divisions *within* ourselves, between the socially acceptable, conforming self that we present to the outside world and the real self that we hide because we're afraid nobody would love us if we showed it.

White parents tend not to be as conscious of all this as BIPOC parents because Whiteness is considered the norm. Ecuadorian parent Melissa recalls her family members making fun of her boyfriends with darker skin and expressing relief when she married a Spanish White husband. Although she didn't want her children to be as White as him (so she wouldn't be mistaken for their nanny), she did want them to have lighter skin than hers because she knew it would ease their path in life.

White parent Liann sees White supremacy showing up in many ways in her life, including in her relentless pursuit of progress on her parenting journey, which means she can never rest. Our culture has taught her (including through her parents' verbal and nonverbal messages) that work must happen before rest or play, and after decades of "pushing through" fatigue, she had internalized the messages that she didn't deserve rest and that her body didn't matter. In her book *Rest Is Resistance*, Tricia Hersey argues that rest is not something we have to earn; it is "not a luxury, a privilege, or a bonus we must wait for once we are burned out." Liann is now learning how resting in her own body allows her to resist White supremacy as she pushes back on the idea that she must always do, produce, and keep moving.

No longer looking for linear progress in her ability to be patient and respond to her children from a place that's aligned with her values (she told me: "I *know* what to do when they scream at me; why can't I *do* it?"), Liann also rests *before* doing chores, cooking, and cleaning, which she says "has offered freedom from resentments unlike anything else ever has." This has given her more capacity to cope with her children's big feelings and to be present with conflict without needing to "fix" it immediately. Liann's partner commented how comfortable she seemed when one of her children got into conflict with another child at the park—acknowledging both children's feelings and stepping back to allow them to handle it when they were able. Liann's rest practices have helped her internalize nourishment and care when feeling hard things, even in the midst of a cluttered house or a tense relational moment.

Rest has also helped to generate more creativity within her family around how they can dismantle White supremacy within their community. For example, they now have dinner with a single BIPOC parent in their neighborhood, either cooking together or taking turns. They're building community across racial lines and sharing labor that would otherwise be done individually. A transgender neighbor needed a car to get to work; Liann's family didn't have extra money, but they used their yard, which has busy street exposure, to host a yard sale and then gave the funds to their neighbor. Through rest, Liann noticed that she had unmet needs for connection and collaboration—and a free evening each week. She has joined a collective that empowers Black families on their pregnancy journeys and pitches in at a local native garden that is a safe space for local Indigenous communities. Spending time in her own garden with her partner has sparked a lot of dreaming—in the short term of sharing their food abundance with others, and in the longer term of working in food and climate justice through regenerative farming—which will likely require as much rest as action.

Because Whiteness is seen as the default and best way of existing in Eurocentric cultures, most psychological research is done on White children and families, and especially middle-class White children and families. Researchers assume that if they remove the stressors of poverty and racism that often accompany non-Whiteness, we'll better understand what children and families are "really" like. So when we see the results of these studies describing a particular intervention resulting in the "best" outcome for children, it often means that it results in the "best" outcome for a small group of middle-class White children to succeed within the constraints of a White supremacist, patriarchal, capitalist system. The researchers assume that if *all* children would only act like the children who achieved these best outcomes, then the broadest benefits would be achieved: which means reducing our dependence on the government but never questioning its authority.

PATRIARCHY PREVENTS US FROM BEING OUR WHOLE SELVES

Even a couple of years ago, I couldn't really have defined "patriarchy" properly—I just assumed it was about middle-aged White men holding all the power in the world. I learned from my (White, cisgender, heterosexual male) friend Brian Stout what patriarchy really is, and also what it does, and that seeing women as the victims and men as the oppressors is part of the game. I paraphrase Dr. Carol Gilligan, who has spent decades writing about patriarchy, and her former student Naomi Snider, who say that patriarchy:

- Leads us to see human capacities as either "masculine" or "feminine," and privileges the masculine.

- Elevates some men (White, cisgender, heterosexual) over other men (BIPOC, homosexual, transgender), and all men over women.

- Forces a split between the self and relationships so that men have selves but women have relationships. Men have power and own their ideas but are emotionally isolated, while women get to have relationships so long as they appear selfless and don't reveal their true ideas if these have the potential to rock the boat.

Even though every person has characteristics that are associated with the masculine and the feminine, the ones associated with masculinity are seen as "better." It's not hard to decipher which list of traits are desirable and rewarded, and which ones are seen as weak and punished (or which traits we punish boys for showing but tolerate in girls) in our culture:

SAMPLE "MASCULINE" TRAITS	SAMPLE "FEMININE" TRAITS
Confidence	Nurturing
Responsibility	Tenderness
Focus	Kindness
Logic	Intuition
Courage	Surrendering

The effects of these characteristics may be less obvious as we navigate school and first jobs, but things begin to shift a little when we partner up—and then shift a lot after our first child is born. Vanishingly few of us talk with our partners early in our relationships about what life will be like after we have children, and because, in heterosexual relationships, the mother is usually making less money and "her natural place is in the home" anyway, she's the one whose career gets put on hold. Maybe she stays out of the workforce long-term (and so devotes herself to the routine of caregiving, laundry, cooking, and playdates), or returns to work and has to balance all of those things plus a fulfilling career (but not *too* fulfilling, since her primary responsibility is, of course, to her family).

Black feminist author bell hooks writes that "male domination has not destroyed the longing men and women have to love one another, even though it makes fulfilling that longing almost impossible to realize." Very often, the wife feels as though she can't talk with the husband about parenting, or even about life beyond her role as a parent. Instead, she becomes a container for the feelings her husband can't process himself: holding the emotional weight of the family, being hyper-attuned to its climate, and pacifying the children so they won't irritate their father into an outburst. This unacknowledged mental load can leave mothers feeling a deep sense of anger—and the *expression* of female anger is not sanctioned within the patriarchal system. Parent Rebecca says she was taught (implicitly) that the mother's job is always to sacrifice for her family. Her mother didn't rest, didn't ask anything for herself, and didn't say no—she would just keep working with anger and resentment simmering in the background, which kept everyone on edge.

All of this male domination happens in partnerships that might have "seemed equal" up until the children arrived, but mothers are not neutral parties in the passing on of patriarchal messages: they actively participate in it. Parent Kate remembers how her relationship with her mother was incredibly strained; her mother's approval and love were dependent on Kate's performance in school and on other tasks, and she wielded shame like a sword. Kate now sees that she didn't know what was important or valuable to *her* because she always needed to keep an eye on her mother to see what *she* valued. In a heart-wrenching conversation in Kate's teenage years, her mother told her that she couldn't love Kate unconditionally because she didn't approve of some of the things Kate did. Kate understands now that this was grounded in the fear that she wouldn't "turn out well" by White supremacist, patriarchal, capitalist standards, and that if her mother loved her, Kate's performance would slip—which would lead to an unfulfilled life. Kate now has to work extra hard to enjoy restful, unproductive time with her child; to communicate her own unconditional love; and to be sure her child knows that it's

OK for her and her child to have different ideas. Again, bell hooks reminds us that if want to heal patriarchal wounds in our culture: "We've got to challenge the way we parent . . . this has to begin on the level of the family."

CAPITALISM FILLS THE HOLES THAT WHITE SUPREMACY AND PATRIARCHY CREATE

Capitalism is, in neutral terms, an economic system where things are owned by people or companies, people make individual decisions about investing, and things are produced, distributed and priced on the free market. A country's success at doing this is measured by its Gross Domestic Product: higher numbers are always better, as they indicate that people are buying more things—said to be a key indicator of wellbeing. Theologian Brian McLaren contradicts this view: "The current extractive economy has nothing to do with actual well-being. In fact, it now has almost everything to do with the loss of well-being . . . Gross Domestic Product is really just a measure of the speed by which we destroy the earth and convert it into money."

In addition to maximum extraction from the earth, capitalism also extracts the maximum from people—paying them as little as possible, and returning a small portion of the excess in charitable good deeds and consolidating political power along with wealth. Historian Dr. Heather Cox Richardson observes that wealthy, educated, well-connected, usually White male leaders argue that "it is important that wealth concentrate in their hands, since they will act as its stewards, using it wisely in lump sums, while if the workers who produce wealth get control of it they will fritter it away." It's an economic model centered on creating wealth for the few at the expense of the many, and the separation of the few and the many through capitalism both reinforces and is reinforced by White supremacy and patriarchy.

Many of us feel an incredible sense of loneliness and disconnection from others (and especially from those without young children!) that has a cause we can't quite pinpoint, but capitalism promises it has the answer for us: consumption. When beauty standards are tightly defined, we need just the right products (removing hair from women's bodies/growing it on men's heads; branded cars, clothes, and phones; engagement rings that cost three months' salary—the product of one of the most effective advertising campaigns ever . . .) to express our uniqueness—even though millions of other people are wearing and using the exact same things to express *their* uniqueness.

Mothers are doing all the research on nannies and day cares and preschools and schools; we're making sure our child gets just the right nutrition while avoiding safety hazards; we're making sure our children have all the right toys and subscription kits to give them the skills they'll need to get ahead in life (Coding! Gymnastics! A second language!). We think that if we can buy the right combination of stuff and expose them to just the right things, they'll be successful—by which we mean "successful in the capitalist system," which involves having a good job and the money to buy anything they reasonably want, and not using the welfare system.

Parent Rebecca wonders what career she would have ended up in if she could have chosen based on what she loved and was good at. As a child, she wanted to be a writer, an actor, and a dancer, but questions from well-meaning teachers and other adults ("But how will you get paid for that?") conveyed the message that these were not "real" jobs.

The problem with capitalism is that there's never enough to go around. Shareholders always want more returns. We always want ("need") more stuff. We always put off dealing with things that *cost* money but don't produce more money or more stuff immediately—things like environmental cleanup, avoiding environmental disasters in the first place, and mitigating climate change. Capitalism treats natural resources as freely available for maximum extraction, often using BIPOC people's labor, with waste products dumped in the water/land/air closest to where BIPOC people live. People in Eurocentric countries are responsible for most of the greenhouse gas emissions that are causing climate change, which primarily affects BIPOC people, but because we're distracted by other things (including making money to buy more stuff), we don't do anything about it. For a long time, White women have seen access to work (and, therefore, money and economic status) as the solution to problems of discrimination—but Black women have not found freedom from sexism or even economic independence in the drudgery of menial work.

When we buy solutions to our problems, we forget how to value the things that make life meaningful but don't have a price tag—things like caring for children and the elderly, walks in nature, and being in community with others. Parent J. D. says that money has provided the illusion of security in his family: his parents accumulated wealth as a substitute for relationships. They saved for every circumstance that might befall them, and for the end of their lives, because they couldn't know that anyone would take care of them. They didn't have the social contracts they needed to rely on other people without paying them. (And yet think of all the people who lost their life savings in a financial downturn, or because a financier created a Ponzi scheme, and who had to go back to work in old age. From this perspective, financial savings may be even riskier than social contracts.)

THE INTERCONNECTION PERPETUATES ALL THREE FACTORS

These three factors—White supremacy, patriarchy, and capitalism—are intricately intertwined in the ways they affect our lives:

- White supremacy upholds White beauty standards, and capitalism sells products to help us meet them.

- Capitalism tells us that resources are limited, so we need to compete to get our share, which makes it easier to use racism (*"they* aren't like us; they're trying to get what should be ours"), and justify more spending (on classes, clubs, sports, subscription boxes, tutoring, test preparation, etc.) to give our child an advantage.

- Patriarchy rewards people with more masculine characteristics and punishes those with more feminine characteristics (except where White women are punished for straying from caring for others by appearing too confident, bossy, and demanding, and Black women are punished for being perceived as "too strong, hard, evil, and castrating"). Capitalism translates this reward system into financial terms by compensating people who choose "masculine"-type careers (science, technology, engineering, math, entrepreneurship, business, etc.) more than people who choose "feminine"-type careers (teaching, nursing, elder care, etc.).

- White supremacy privileges able bodies: everything about our homes, communities, schools, and systems are designed for able-bodied people (with minimal accommodations provided by the Americans with Disabilities Act). Parents who are fortunate to have excess time and resources can fight for accommodations for their children and themselves; school districts and companies argue that providing environments where everyone can meet their full potential is too expensive.

- Patriarchal power flows downhill. The father in a heterosexual relationship signals his power by refusing to get overinvolved in issues related to parenting, leaving the mother to manage the household. Older children see their lack of power and take it out on younger children, or the dog. Parents sense the disconnection with their children and buy them gifts in an unsuccessful attempt to bridge the gap.

Because we're all swimming in this toxic soup, it can be incredibly difficult to even see it for what it is, never mind knowing what to do about it or actually doing something risky about it (at the potential cost of our social standing among relatives, friends, and colleagues). There is so much to do that it can feel like we'll *never* heal our individual selves or our broader culture from all of these factors.

But we *can* start to do things differently, and to heal. We can take one small step, and then follow that with another small step. These small steps can happen in our homes and in our interactions with our children. We can see our children's resistance against our attempts to control them for what it is—an assertion of their needs, an assertion that we used to make as well before our parents and teachers trained us to stuff down our feelings and ignore our needs.

This book is about seeing the real reasons why parenting is so hard: because we're trying to heal from the traumas that White supremacy, patriarchy, and capitalism have wreaked on us at the same time as they continue to damage our relationships with our children—whether we identify as White or BIPOC.

By treating your own child with respect for who they really are, you will make a massive difference in their life; this is a way of interacting that your parents could never even have imagined because patriarchy taught them they had to be in charge and in control at all times.

Parents can try to heal White supremacy by teaching children that every person (in fact, every living and nonliving thing as well) deserves our respect simply by existing.

Finding such a sense of *right*-ness, self-acceptance, and self-compassion means that our children won't need to buy endless piles of stuff to assuage the loneliness and emptiness they feel inside.

COMPLIANCE ISN'T OUR GOAL

Most parenting advice is about how to get children to comply with our wishes—and preferably to give them a false sense of control by making them think the compliance was their idea ("Would you like the blue toothbrush or the red one?"). But in this book, *compliance is not our goal.* We can't expect to raise a child who will completely obey us until they're eighteen and then suddenly know how to be in healthy relationships with boundaries and stand up against the wrongs they see in the world.

If we care about raising children with a real moral compass, we have to start that process *now.* But that doesn't mean we're just going to let our child walk all over us! Our first step is to set aside the idea that our way of doing things is the right way, or even the only way. When we're focused on this, we use our power over our child to get them to do what we want them to do. Instead, this book will show you how to be in a respectful relationship with your child—and not the *obedience* kind of respect we were raised with but respect that acknowledges both parent *and* child have needs in their relationship, and that both of these sets of needs can be met.

IT ALL COMES DOWN TO NEEDS

All people have needs. You might have a core set of needs that you're trying to meet most of the time—this will be different for each person but might include things like connection with your child and your partner (if you have one), self-care, rest, respect, and growth/learning, plus others that pop up from time to time like empathy, sexual expression, choice, celebration, and mourning. (There's a broader List of Needs on page 208, and you may find it helpful to write down or highlight which needs you are trying to meet most often on the needs cupcake template on page 211. I'll walk you through this in Chapter 4.)

Your child has needs too: basic needs like nourishment and rest, as well as emotional safety and connection with their primary caregiver, closely followed by the needs to be truly known and for autonomy, joy, discovery, and movement. Some children may prioritize different needs that we'll discuss later in the book, but this is a good starting point.

When our needs are met, we tend to feel "right" in the world— satisfied, joyful, and at ease. When they aren't, we feel "not right"—sometimes we feel this in our emotions, perhaps uneasy, resentful, or angry. Sometimes we feel it in our bodies—tension in our shoulders, a lump in our throat, holding our breath without realizing it, nausea—although we may have been covering up these signals for so long that we don't always notice them anymore. White supremacy, patriarchy, and capitalism combine like a poison to keep us from getting our needs met as whole people in our families, which also keeps these forces in business.

ASSERTING (AND DENYING) NEEDS

Our children know their needs, and they aren't shy about asserting them! Very often, we find ourselves feeling flooded by our child's behavior when they do age-appropriate things like refusing to brush their teeth, making a mess, and not using appropriate manners.

FLOODED VERSUS TRIGGERED

When you feel a big reaction that's out of proportion to your child's behavior, it's called being flooded. If the current event reminds you of past trauma you've experienced, then we can say you're feeling triggered. Being flooded and being triggered are both a form of dysregulation, which extends before and after the triggered/flooded sensation. Think of the dysregulation as the clouds and rain that occur before, during, and after the lightning storm of the triggered/flooded feelings.

We once knew what our own needs were as well, and told our parents and caregivers about them—but when we did this, we were often punished and shamed. We were instructed to be quiet, to stop making such a fuss, to do what we were told. Our job was to do well in school, get a good job, get married, buy a house . . . and more stuff. Even if your parents told you to "follow your dreams" on the career front, that may have been within defined parameters of sexuality, emotional expression, and behavior. The parents at the top of the family hold all the power, with the child fighting to be heard (patriarchy), with one path in life considered to be "correct" and any deviation from that representing a failure (White supremacy), the whole thing designed to keep us earning money and buying stuff (capitalism).

Remember how connection and safety may be your child's top needs? This means that when we threaten to remove their connection with us (e.g., by using time-outs or other punishments) or their emotional or physical safety (yelling, spanking), the child finds this an impossibly difficult situation. A child who has really strong needs to be truly known, and for autonomy, discovery, joy, and movement, may keep asserting these needs—these are children we call defiant and problematic. We double down on our efforts to shape their behavior into something that meets *our* needs. If we're successful, the child learns that they must disregard their needs to preserve their connection with us. When their behavior meets our approval, we'll give them the connection and emotional safety they crave—so they split off the part of themselves that needed to be known, autonomous, etc., and pretend those needs don't exist anymore.

In a podcast interview, parent Amy described how she was a spirited child who was too much for her parents to cope with. She was shamed for always wanting to have the last word; her parents told her: "Someday you'll make a great prosecutor!" Her need to be heard might be monetizable one day, but it was an undesirable quality in a chaotic, volatile family headed by overwhelmed parents.

We spend so many decades suppressing our needs that much of the time we have no idea what they are! Parent Stephanie told me that before she started working with me, she "didn't even know what it meant to have a need."

The facing page shows a diagram illustrating how this works in our families.

Let's take a closer look at the ways that these forces show up in our families, and how we keep them going through our interactions inside our family and with the wider world.

PARENTING UNDER WHITE SUPREMACY, PATRIARCHY, AND CAPITALISM

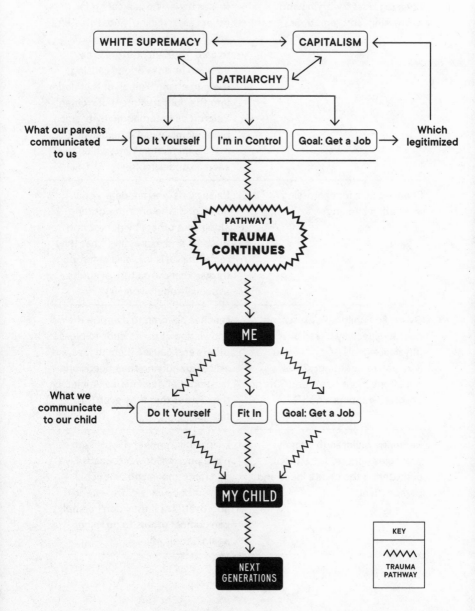

ACTION	WHAT EFFECT THIS ACTION HAS ON A CHILD
Shaming boys for crying and expressing "soft" emotions.	Raises boys who see caring for others as "feminine" and distasteful and cannot truly allow others to care for them or express any emotion besides anger, causing them to channel much of that anger into the poor treatment of women. Reinforces heteronormativity since being homosexual is perceived to make a man effeminate, which is seen as undesirable.
Shaming girls for expressing frustration and anger.	Raises girls who are deferential, quiet, and who prioritize getting along with others by not rocking the boat and expressing what they really think. (This is also enforced through cancel culture of adults, especially adult women.)
Overriding children's expressed needs, especially based on physical signals (e.g., "Are you sure you're not hungry? How about one more bite?" and "Oh, go on, give Grandma a hug.")	Teaches children to override their knowledge of their needs to please others and causes them to lose the skill of identifying their needs and trusting their feelings, so ultimately they forget that they even have needs.
Requiring children to comply with rules parents set without considering the child's ideas and perspective.	Trains children that people with more physical power (because we can force them) and emotional power (because we can withhold approval/love if they don't comply) can compel others to do things against their will.

ACTION	WHAT EFFECT THIS ACTION HAS ON A CHILD
Giving time-outs and other punishments for "bad behavior."	Lets our children know that we can't cope with their difficult feelings; that we will give them connection, love, and approval when their behavior matches our expectations; and creates a lasting fear that others will not accept the child (and later adult) if they express the full range of their feelings.
Wanting a child (especially a girl) to always be happy, rather than experiencing the full range of human feelings.	Forces our children to stuff down their "undesirable" feelings and only display the ones that please and reassure us.
Requiring that children learn to express themselves verbally ("Use your words!") and to cooperate after the parent explains the logic of what is clearly the best way to do things.	Confirms that only the person in authority knows the right way to do things and how to communicate, and implies others must communicate in a way that's most convenient for that person and do what the authority figure wants.
Encouraging a child's independence and separation from parents (when starting day care, school, and daily life).	Tells children they must be self-sufficient at all costs and not show neediness by asking for help from others.
Sharing resources (lists of preschools with openings; lists of schools with admissions criteria, etc.) with groups of parents who are "like us."	Enforces racial segregation and perpetuates children only feeling comfortable with others of their own racial and/or socioeconomic identity.

ACTION	WHAT EFFECT THIS ACTION HAS ON A CHILD
Moving to a neighborhood because it has "good schools" (with ratings driven by test scores, which are a proxy for the number of BIPOC students present), and devising ratings schemes so all families know which schools have the most resources.	Hoards resources to make them primarily available to White children, with limited numbers of BIPOC children allowed to be present as long as it benefits White children by "exposing them to diversity" and doesn't cause White children to feel "out of place."
Advocating for resources in school to benefit our children (second languages, lacrosse, coding, etc.) without considering what resources *all* children in the school need.	Ensures that our children have the resources they need to "get ahead."
Demonstrating traditional gender roles. Father works, yells at the children when they don't comply, plays ball with them. Mother's job is seen as less important; she does all the research on parenting, cooks the meals, and takes care of the kids when they're sick, even when she has a job. She used to yell when she felt angry but has been learning self-regulation skills because she feels guilty after yelling, and now she manages the emotional climate of the family.	Teaches children who should perform each role and the relative values of each role. Attuning to the children is women's work, so there's no need for a father to learn more effective communication methods. A mother's work may be romanticized as important, but under capitalist rules, unpaid work will always be subservient to paid work.
Attending the most prestigious schools, providing tutoring, preparing children to attend elite universities.	Secures resources that are perceived to be scarce for our child so our child can continue to accumulate wealth.

ACTION	WHAT EFFECT THIS ACTION HAS ON A CHILD
Rewarding girls who exhibit "masculine"-type characteristics like bravery, courage, risk-taking.	Overvalues "masculine" emotional characteristics and deemphasizes "feminine" emotional characteristics.
Encouraging girls to pursue science, technology, engineering, and math (STEM)-related careers but discouraging both boys and girls from considering caring-based careers like teaching and nursing.	Overvalues the role of "masculine"-type careers and minimizes the role of "feminine"-type careers.
Being "color blind" and not teaching children explicitly about bias and racism because "we don't want to scare them" and "we're not racist anyway; we treat everyone the same."	Teaches our children that race is an important characteristic to define people, that we're afraid of discussing it, and that they can treat other people differently based on their race and we probably won't find out or correct them.
Being unaware of the ways we reinforce Eurocentric cultural dominance through practices like insisting on "proper" pronunciation and grammar, seeing typically White facial and body features as more beautiful, and privileging heteronormative family structures.	Teaches children to unquestioningly comply with White supremacist norms at the expense of their own full expression as human beings and to enforce other people's compliance with these norms as well.
Relying on "chains of care" of BIPOC women who must spend time apart from their own children to care for White and privileged children.	Helps White parents to secure resources for some children at the expense of other families' abilities to be present for each other.

It can seem that the best path forward is to get everyone what White men currently have right now, which may look from the outside like a whole lot of freedom and privilege. After all, if there are going to be people who are dominated and people who do the dominating, wouldn't it be better—*Lean In* style—to be the latter than the former? This view assumes that White cisgender heterosexual men have it pretty great right now, and the reality is that they don't. Patriarchy is killing them about as much as it's killing White women, although perhaps not as much as BIPOC people.

Right now, White cisgender heterosexual men do most of the dominating, but the solution isn't to give everyone their same privileges so everyone dominates. The solution is to heal ourselves and our families so the dominate/be dominated mindset is no longer valid, and instead, we work to meet everyone's needs. I do want to be clear that parents are not the only people responsible for these social challenges, and families are not the only place where they will be solved. We need all people to advocate for new policies that dismantle these systems that are hurting *all* of us. There are some suggestions on page 204 for ways you can participate in these actions.

Two important ideas remain: Firstly, if we focus only on the structural changes in the wider world but we don't address what's happening in families, we won't be successful at creating a society in which everyone can be their true selves. We need both things to happen.

Secondly, our young children *already know* how to be their true selves. They understand and advocate for their needs, and while they don't always do it perfectly because their brains are still developing, they get it right far more often than we give them credit for. We may remember how *we* desperately needed to be heard when we were children but were socialized to "be quiet." How many times have we told our own children to stop advocating for their own needs and to just do what we tell them to do? I know I've done it a whole lot of times when it comes down to getting teeth brushed, getting into bed, and getting out of the house. It happens much less often now that I have new tools to navigate these kinds of situations.

Each time we interact with our children, especially in the difficult moments, we get to decide whether we will socialize them into racist, patriarchal, capitalist systems, or whether we will work with them to forge a different path, one where all people's needs are seen and respected. These ideas aren't new; they're deeply grounded in the kinds of relationships Indigenous parents used to have with their children before White people tried to kill and then assimilate them, and they still have these relationships where they've been able to continue these practices. Miranda, a First Nations parent with whom I work, once described her parenting approach (which is grounded in the methods described in this book) to her great-aunt, who responded: "Oh yes; those are the old ways." Miranda explained this to me as: "That's how we used to raise children before the residential school system existed. Child-rearing was kind and collaborative and respect for all things was an integral part of life." If we don't identify as Indigenous, our job is not to appropriate knowledge that doesn't belong to us but to recognize its validity and create our own path based on an ethic of respect for all people and for the earth.

The following page illustrates what that might look like.

PARENTING IN A SOCIETY HEALING FROM WHITE SUPREMACY, PATRIARCHY, AND CAPITALISM

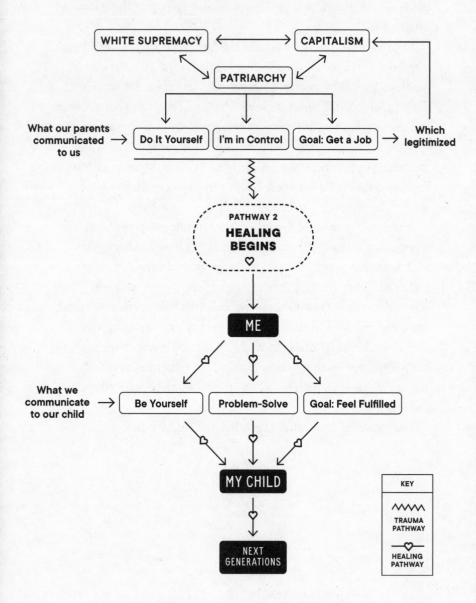

Parenting Beyond Power, by Jen Lumanlan © 2023

You may worry that listening to and meeting your child's needs is going to turn you into a permissive parent whose child runs the show, but that won't happen because we're also going to look at how to meet *your* needs—and when both people's needs are met in a relationship, the concepts of "strictness" and "permissiveness" become irrelevant. There are just two people who feel fulfilled because both of their needs are satisfied. And then most of the challenges you're facing with "bad behavior," like answering back, fighting between siblings, resisting, stalling, and everything else that your child does that drives you up the wall, fall away as well.

At the end of the day, we may find that we've done two things. We have created a joy-filled, respect-based relationship with our children, who are in mutually satisfying relationships with us. And we have the best chance of raising children who treat *all* people with dignity and respect—because it'll just be part of the fabric of how they live their lives. It's a practice of actively moving toward the kind of culture we want to see in the world by living it every day in our families.

CHAPTER 2:

JUDGMENTS, REWARDS, AND PUNISHMENTS

They "Work" (But Not the Way We Want Them To)

Respectful parenting isn't that hard when things are going well; when we ask our child to wash their hands, and they willingly trot on down to the bathroom, we can give ourselves a little mental high-five and think: *Go me! I've got this respect thing* down*!*

But it's another story when our child resists. What the heck are we supposed to do when that happens?

Perhaps the first thing you say is something that expresses your exasperation, which comes out as a judgment:

"Why can't you ever just *do what I ask*?"

"Why do *I* have to do this? You're old enough to do it by yourself."

"Why can't you be more like [insert name of sibling/cousin/friend]?"

We can tell we're making a judgment when we use phrases like: "You always . . . ," "You never . . . ," and "You are . . ." In each case, we're imposing our view of the truth on the other person, and not allowing space for their view of it. When people do that to us, it immediately puts us on the defensive and doesn't make us want to collaborate with them. The same is true for our child.

EXERCISE

Set a timer for five minutes and start writing in a notebook using the following prompts. If you finish before the end of five minutes, start from the beginning and do it again to see what comes out differently the second time.

- Think of a time when you felt judged—by a parent, partner, colleague, etc. What did they say? How did you feel afterward? Did it make you want to hear and understand their point of view and collaborate with them on finding a solution to the issue that would work for both of you?
- Think of a time when you judged someone else—your child, partner, colleague, etc. (This includes things you've said in your head or to other people about someone, even if you wouldn't say it to them directly, such as: "My child is so stubborn/defiant/obnoxious.") What was the person's reaction to your words? Or what would it have been, if you had said it to them?

Your go-to approach in difficult situations may be to reward your child for doing what you want (or not doing what you don't want):

"If you tidy your room, we can play a game together!"

"If you brush your teeth, we'll read stories!"

"If you stop crying, you can have a cookie!"

EXERCISE

- What were you rewarded for doing as a child? Do you still do and enjoy this activity today? My husband was paid twenty dollars for every A in high school. He earned mostly As, but he only studied for the purpose of getting the money, and this book is the first one he's read in the eighteen years I've known him.
- What kinds of activities do you reward your child for doing? What rewards do you use? How do you feel about rewards right now? Even if it seems like they are effective, how does it feel when you see your child cooperating to get a reward (perhaps underneath the relief that this isn't going to be yet another fight)? You might want to revisit these questions after you've finished reading this chapter.

When rewards fail, then come the threats and punishments:

"If you don't tidy your room, you can't go to the party on Saturday."

"If you won't brush your teeth, we're not reading stories for the rest of the week."

"If you don't stop crying *right this minute,* I'm going to give you something to *really* cry about."

EXERCISE

- What do you punish your child for doing? What kinds of punishments do you give out, and how does your child respond? Has the punishment "worked" to change your child's behavior? Why do you think this is? How do you feel when you use these punishments?
- Even if you think you don't reward or punish your child often, how often do you use sentences that start: "If you . . ." or "If you don't . . ."? Those are key signs that what follows will require your child to do something (or not do something) to get approval (or avoid being punished).

And you might think: *Well, my parents talked to me like that, and I turned out OK . . . what's wrong with judgments, rewards, and punishments?*

Then I'd invite you to pause and check in for a minute: Did you really "turn out OK"?

Are there big parts of yourself that you hide from other people because you worry they won't like (or love) you if they knew about them?

How is your relationship with your parents? Did you feel judged by them as a child? Do you still feel judged by them now? Do you believe you have to earn their approval? Is this the kind of relationship you want to have with your own child when they're an adult . . . or even now?

We judge people all the time, and it becomes so much a part of our daily lives that we might not even realize it—even though we hate being judged ourselves. We know there's usually a reason why *we* do the thing we do—we're not messy; we just value other activities more than a tidy house—but we don't stop to look at why other people are doing the things *they* do. We assume that their behavior is the only thing that matters, instead of the underlying reasons—and we label them (messy, lazy, defiant) to try to shame them into complying. We do this with both the adults and children in our lives because it's the way of interacting with people that was modeled for us. Judgments are also a key driver of bias; we quickly judge a person to be "like us" or "not like us." Sociologist Michael Kimmel writes: "Judging is how we compare people's performance and evaluate whether a person is reaching an ideal" (related to masculinity, femininity, race, etc.).

When we're tempted to judge or shame another person, one way to avoid doing so is to simply say what you see as if you were a video camera recording the scene. A video camera doesn't record "a mess"; it sees "toys on the floor." Instead of a "lazy" child, it sees a child who isn't setting the table right now. Instead of "defiance," it sees a child who disagrees with their parent. *Observing* a child's behavior, rather than judging it, is the first step toward them wanting to work with you to find a solution to the problem you have together, instead of shutting you down (ignoring you, walking away) because they don't want to feel ashamed.

EXERCISE

Look back to what you wrote in response to the first set of exercises about judging someone's behavior. Now, how could you have phrased it in a way that allowed you to observe the situation (imagine you're a video camera) rather than judge it, and then invite the other person to help you address the issue? You might say something like: "I've noticed that you don't always get dressed in the morning right after breakfast; would you be willing to talk about that?" or "We seem to be having a hard time getting out the door in the mornings; can we talk about it?" Both statements avoid blaming any person for what's happening and invite the other person into the conversation.

PUNISHMENTS AND REWARDS . . .
OPPOSITE SIDES OF THE SAME COIN

So, having read this far, you might be thinking: *I know punishments and judgments are bad, so I'll try and stop using them. I like rewards much better anyway, and my child really responds to them.*

Even though rewards feel good (and they're very much tied to the White Protestant work ethic of self-control and toeing the line until the Ultimate Reward of entry into heaven is achieved), they're really just another side of the punishment coin. Either way, we're telling our child: "I don't like/trust who you are/what you're doing right now, so I'm going to tell you how to change." If we choose punishments, we impose these for noncompliance. When we use rewards, we still put ourselves in the position of judging the child's compliance with our standard before granting the reward.

Rewards can be quite effective at changing the child's behavior because you're usually using them in situations where the child isn't feeling flooded, so they can make a rational choice. And since you know all too well what lights up their little pleasure receptors brighter than the sun, you know how to pick something they'll really want (Stickers! Candy! Screen time!) to tip the scales in your favor. They seem like they're cooperating willingly, so it *seems* more like a win to us . . . but underneath, they still have a need that they are covering up to get the reward.

UNDERSTANDING INTRINSIC MOTIVATION

When we're intrinsically motivated to do something, it means we're doing it because we want to do it, not because the act of doing the thing is rewarded. Parents often want their child to be intrinsically motivated to do chores, which misunderstands the concept. Some children genuinely enjoy tidying up—they are intrinsically motivated. Others may never be intrinsically motivated to tidy up, but they may still be quite happy to work with you and do it together, even if they refuse to do it alone. Their motivation is extrinsic—it's located in the relationship, rather than in themselves, but that's OK as long as they're collaborating willingly. If they still don't want to help, then one solution is to have fewer toys . . .

Rewards and punishments are examples of extrinsic motivators: things we want to make happen (a clean kitchen, a payday) or avoid happening (dental cavities; fines for not paying taxes). Extrinsic motivation will always play a role in our lives, but there's a big difference between rewarding yourself and being rewarded by others. I still reward myself by taking a break after I clear my inbox because clearing my inbox isn't intrinsically rewarding to me. But most of us are happiest when we spend the majority of our time doing things that we find intrinsically rewarding or where we choose our own rewards, rather than when other people are imposing these on us—and it's the same for our children.

Here's the thing: there's plenty of peer-reviewed evidence showing that judgments, rewards, and punishments do "work" to change a child's behavior. Children crave love and attention, and by offering and withholding these, we are using our power to get them to comply with our wishes. The challenge with doing this is that the research also shows that rewards decrease a child's intrinsic motivation to do something. So when we reward children for doing things like eating their vegetables and for sharing with a sibling, we may increase the likelihood they'll do those things in the short term—for as long as we keep rewarding them. Once we cut off the rewards, they're going to be much less willing to do these things than they were before because they stopped being intrinsically motivated and are now only extrinsically motivated to do them.

When we use rewards (or punishments!) to change a child's behavior, we're essentially telling them: "I don't care what your needs are; mine are more important." And pretty often, we find ourselves overwhelmed when they do the very things we were punished for doing as a child. Parent Rebecca's daughter sometimes shouts: "I hate you! I hate you! I hate you!" Rebecca was spanked for saying that as a child because it was "as bad as a swear word," but she remembers she would only say it when she felt incredibly disconnected from and unloved by her parents. She needed connection and love but received punishment instead: she feels triggered when her own child repeats this behavior, and she has to walk away to take a break so as not to snap at her child. Now she sees that when her daughter says "I hate you," she often means something like: "I'm worried that you love my younger brother more than me!" Rebecca makes the mental rephrase, which removes the sting from her daughter's words, and then she's able to reconnect and repair based on the child's real need: for the same connection that she once needed herself.

Think about how you feel when you're having a fight with your partner and they say something that cuts you to the core (whether they meant it to or not). Maybe you explode (yell, slam a door) in that moment, escape (leave the room, mentally shut down), freeze, or try to placate them so they'll stop. Bring that feeling to mind . . . and now imagine that your partner said: "Oh, calm down. It isn't that big of a deal. If you don't stop crying and put your shoes on, you can't watch TV for the rest of the week." Or even: "If you stop crying and put your shoes on, you can have an ice cream."

When you put it like that, it sounds ridiculous, right? How could losing TV privileges (or being promised an ice cream) help you to react differently in the moment, or help you feel a sense of closeness with your partner? Don't forget that when you and your partner fight, you probably have at least one friend you can call to vent to, find perspective, and get moral support. Your child doesn't have anyone else: very often, the person who "caused" their upset (in their mind) is also the only person from whom they can find comfort.

Whenever we punish a child, we're saying: "I don't approve of what you're doing, so I'm going to withhold my approval (and do something else I know you don't like) until you meet my needs." The logic gets even more warped when we spank them for hitting us or someone else: "Hitting is bad!" Spank! "Don't ever hit me/your sibling/the kid at school again!" Spank! In this case, it isn't surprising that the child is confused by the mixed messaging. For some children, the fear of being spanked again is enough to change their behavior. For others, we see that "shit rolls downhill"—the child might stop hitting the parent, but they start hitting a smaller sibling or the family pet.

Researcher and author Brené Brown says: "So many of us are better at inflicting pain than we are at feeling it. We push hurt onto others rather than turning toward it and feeling our way through the darkness." Rather than continuing to push our pain onto our child, it's our job to heal the pain so we can show up differently for our child.

The key here is to see that your child isn't hitting you, resisting you, or being defiant because they want to hit you; they're hitting you because they have a need that isn't being met (we'll learn much more about this in Chapter 4), and they don't know how to express that need—or they've tried to express it, and you've told them you can't or won't accommodate it.

Parent Masako's son was born with a rare skin condition, and he must take a bath every day to make sure his skin stays moisturized. Masako's husband would usually be the one to give the bath, and her son would resist at every step of the way. Bath time was becoming stressful for the whole family as they went through the nightly dance of cajoling, running away, and tears. Here it might seem like the thing to "fix" is how to get the child in the bath, but Masako realized that her child's difficult behavior was actually an indicator of unmet needs for connection with her, and for autonomy (he wants some say over what happens to his body, even though he must take a bath). Now she and her son play together for five minutes before bath time, and they've instituted a safe word ("bananas") that means "stop." The first night, her son said it every thirty seconds to test whether it would work. (It did.) Then he was able to use it to say things like: "the water is too hot/cold" and "I don't like water on my face." She also realized that she and her husband had some unprocessed feelings from when the skin condition was diagnosed at the time of her son's birth, which meant that bath time was emotionally charged for both parents. This often led to bickering, and to her son being afraid that bath time would lead to a fight between his parents. Now that Masako and her husband have talked through their feelings and identified and met everyone's needs, bath time is fun and easy—all because Masako learned how to see beneath the signal of her child's "difficult" behavior.

EXERCISE

Bring to mind something you have a hard time with right now. It might be related to the way you interact with your partner or how you feel about your body or your parenting. What makes this hard for you? Have you told anyone that you're close to how you're feeling? If not, why not? If you have, did you get a reaction that felt connecting to you?

Now think back to your childhood: What did your parents say about this when you were growing up? If you crumple when your partner is even slightly critical, can you remember back to feeling judged as a child? If you're ashamed of your body now, did this come from judgments (or maybe even rewards or punishments) related to your body or to food as a child? If you feel that you must do everything perfectly as a parent, did you learn that you must be perfect as a child? You might want to do some journaling on these questions.

Another parent, Cassie, rewarded her children with screen time and candy for doing things like picking up toys and pooping on the potty (with a child who was refusing due to a power struggle), even though her own training as a psychologist made her hesitant to do this. She then shifted to using sticker charts with prizes for issues where she didn't care whether they developed intrinsic motivation— like not screaming when they get their hair wet in the shower. Her daughter exchanged stickers for a trip to the zoo, and Cassie passed over a note card with a script to the ticket booth person, who would say, "I need to see your reservation and a full sticker chart, please." Cassie saw her daughter's pride as she pulled the sticker chart out of her purse for the ticket booth person to "scan" and as the rest of the family thanked her for "treating" them to a day at the zoo.

Through our work together, Cassie realized what children *really* learn when we reward them. They learn something about the activity we're rewarding them for, like whether they should override the need that's causing them to scream in the shower—which might be a fear that they'll get shampoo in their eyes, or that the temperature isn't right, or that they don't like water running down their face. But they're also learning something about their relationship with us. They learn that we are in a position of power, and we get to judge their behavior and deem it acceptable or not acceptable. When it's acceptable, we reward. When it's not, we don't. The desire for the stickers, the day at the zoo, and her mother's approval were sometimes successful at getting Cassie's daughter to stop screaming in the shower. Her children are strong-willed, and rewards didn't always "work"—in other words, they were able to stay in touch with their needs and prioritize them some of the time. Children who are more reliant on a parent's approval will go for the rewards, often to the parent's relief, but at the expense of truly being seen and understood.

After she decided to move away from rewards, Cassie quickly realized that rewards are a lot easier in the short term—it does take mental effort to learn and practice a new tool, especially when you're dysregulated a lot of the time yourself! But a couple weeks after starting to use the methods in this book, Cassie told me: "The positive side is (and I am not exaggerating) the kids now have *zero* meltdowns or tantrums with me. It's really remarkable. They've been waiting their whole lives for someone to listen to them! All fifty and thirty months of it, respectively."

Now think about how many different things you punish your child for, or how many times you punish them for the same infraction, and know that each and every time this happens, the child learns: "My parent doesn't accept me for who I am. I'll put a wall around this need I have that they find unacceptable because my need to feel loved by them is greater than that other need." When we do this over and over, day in and day out, the real lesson our children are learning is not "how to not scream in the shower/make a mess/hit my sibling" but how to suppress what's really important to them so they can get someone else's approval.

Cassie very much wanted to stop rewarding and punishing her children, but she felt like she was in a "parenting behavior vacuum" because she wasn't well versed enough on what she *should* be doing. She felt paralyzed and unable to do something different because she wasn't sure that any other method would result in less stress for her at home. Once she started using the Problem-Solving Approach, she was shocked at how effective it was—even with her two-year-old son, which she didn't expect at all because he's barely verbal.

That's not to say that this has been a completely easy transition for Cassie. Think about when you learned a new skill that you're now really good at: there was a time when it wasn't easy at all. Maybe you doubted your ability to do the thing at all, but you stuck with it, and the more you practiced, the easier it became. Or think about parenting an infant: *That* wasn't easy either, right? You had to learn a new person's needs when they couldn't even speak, and their main communication method was crying.

But eventually you learned when your baby's cries meant: "I'll be asleep again in five minutes" or "I need help *now*!" When you keep using the Problem-Solving Approach, you don't have to remember a complete script of "the thing you're supposed to say in difficult moments." You don't have to stuff your feelings down and pretend you're not feeling frustrated when you really are. It's OK to feel, and even say: "I'm feeling frustrated right now!" When you do this, you'll probably find the feeling dissipates fairly quickly, leaving you more able to respond to your child with empathy. And you don't have to coerce your child against their will—they'll start telling you their needs and proposing solutions to problems between you that actually meet both of your needs, which takes the burden off you.

WHAT ABOUT CONSEQUENCES?

I see a lot of parents confused about whether and how to use consequences. There are two kinds of consequences: natural and logical.
A natural consequence happens without any decision by the parent:
if the child goes out without a jacket when it's freezing outside, they
may get cold. Natural consequences are a normal part of life, and
we don't need to shield our child from them (although we might
consider being benevolent the first few times and bring the jacket
along for the walk).

An adult creates a logical consequence, which often starts with
the words: "If you don't . . ." For example: "If you don't brush your
teeth soon, we won't have time for stories before bed." Logical
consequences establish a power relationship that says: "When your
behavior meets my wishes, you can have what you want." Logical
consequences are essentially a form of punishment and put you in a
position of power over your child. The more often you use them, the
less likely your child is going to want to work toward meeting both
of your needs. If you must use them, try to do so sparingly, immediately after the incident, and make the consequence relevant to the
child's action. Not having time for stories before bed if teeth aren't
brushed soon is an appropriate logical consequence—but because
we haven't identified the child's needs, the same issue will likely
recur tomorrow. Over the next few chapters we'll learn creative
ways to meet your needs and your child's needs to get us out of this
cycle—perhaps in this case by reading stories while brushing teeth.

Parents are drawn to "logical" consequences (which I put in
quotation marks because, most of the time, they really aren't very
logical). This is because it seems like a good way to induce compliance without actually punishing our child, and also because we *want*
our children to be logical and respond to logic. But logical consequences really *are* punishment.

LAYING THE FOUNDATION FOR FUTURE SUCCESS

When we're using judgments, rewards, and punishments, we're trying to change the child's behavior. Perhaps you're thinking: *Well, duh ... of course, I'm trying to get my child to stop smearing poop on the carpet/smacking their sibling/talking back to me.* Changing someone's behavior is not only really hard but builds up walls between us and them.

Think about how many times you've already rewarded or punished them for doing or not doing the thing you want them to do *right now.* Do you get the sense that they're changing their behavior because they've seen the error of their ways and now believe that your way really is better? Or do they mostly do a good enough job to get the reward/avoid the punishment, and then, when they know your back is turned, do they do it the old way if they can? If so, that's how you know they're extrinsically motivated; they're only changing their behavior because they want your approval.

I'm not saying that all rewards are terrible. In fact, we all use them all the time. Many of us work outside the home for the reward of money that we can use to buy the things we need and want. We get rewards from credit card companies, supermarkets, video games, the classes we take, and from our boss at work. These rewards are all designed to get us to do more of something: spend more money, rack up more points, learn something new, do something our employer wants us to do. And there's nothing wrong with being aware of these kinds of systems and using them to our and our child's advantage! My daughter is learning to read using an app that rewards her with sixty seconds of a race-car game when she's completed exercises, and she says to me: "I'm doing the reward now!" Not using rewards in our relationship with our child doesn't mean they won't be able to work in systems where they are rewarded.

There are two key differences, however, between being an adult in these situations where rewards are used and us rewarding our child. Firstly, as adults, we have fully developed brains and can understand the choice we're making. Secondly, nobody is offering us more of something that's so absolutely central to our well-being as a parent's love and affection.

A child isn't born with a fully developed brain. When they're very young, they aren't able to think through all of the implications of their decisions, or plan ahead, or remember what happened the last time they tried something. When they're making a decision about whether to accept a reward, they're making it purely based on what would feel good right now, so putting other needs on hold to get candy or screen time is hardly even a choice. They aren't consciously deciding to put their own needs on hold to meet yours, and we're using their inability to do this to get them to comply with something they *know* doesn't meet their needs.

They may well have very valid needs that aren't being met by the thing we're asking them to do. Taking potty training as an example: the child might not want to use the potty because they're afraid of it, or they don't like being cold when they take their pants off, or they are enjoying playing and don't want to stop, or they want to be close to you and not separated from you in the bathroom. If all we focus on is changing their behavior (by rewarding them for pooping in the potty), the child learns to ignore and override what their bodies are telling them and what they know they need because they want the reward. If we have already rewarded our child for using the potty, then this alone hasn't "broken" them or our relationship, but it does set the tone for the kinds of interactions we're going to have with our child: the kind where we manipulate them into doing things we want them to do.

So many of our struggles as adults come from knowing that we are not accepted for our full selves. We bury all the parts of us that our parents wouldn't (or couldn't) accept—our creativity, our exuberance, our selfishness, our sexuality—and pretend it's not as important to us as it really is (until perhaps we can't bear to live with the split in ourselves any longer). And when we reward our children for overriding their needs to meet our needs, we're setting our children up to struggle in the exact same ways that we have struggled.

If we have a goal of raising children who will go out into the world and stand up for their values, they need practice at doing this while they're still young. One of the things that most of the few thousand Germans who helped Jewish people escape persecution during the Holocaust had in common (out of the nine million who could have helped) was that rescuers were more likely to have been raised to behave in ways that were aligned with their values and question rules that weren't. They could think for themselves and act independently based on their convictions, rather than following the herd. They were also more likely to have known somebody in childhood who went out of their way to help others, and to not draw lines between "people like us" and "those not like us," which shows that what we model is just as important as what we teach.

When we judge our child's behavior, even if we only use this language in our heads, we allow their behavior to control us. When we think: "My child is so messy/rude/defiant," we link their actual behavior (leaving toys out/speaking to us in a tone we don't like/ turning away when we talk to them) with stories from our own childhoods about the difficult experiences we've had: "Messy children will never learn to be responsible." "Rude children won't be able to function in the world." "Defiance can't be tolerated." This creates big feelings in us! We're experiencing pain because we want our children to be successful, and we look for someone to blame. It seems like the only path forward is to get our child to cooperate—it's for their own good, after all, right? But when we can shift our language and approach their actions without judgment, we remove the power of things outside of ourselves to define our experience, which can create a sense of empathy and compassion—both for ourselves and for our child.

When we move beyond using judgments, rewards, and punishments, we offer our children the chance to have a relationship with us as they truly are—which sets the stage for them to feel seen and understood in their whole selves. This can be hard for us because, most likely, we were never fully seen ourselves as children, so we may not even know what it feels like. There's a danger that we may go too far the other way by ignoring our own needs as parents in service of our children. When that happens, we stray into permissive parenting—and this is not where we want to be. That's a recipe for frustration and resentment as your child's needs get met and yours are ignored. Don't worry; there is lots of help coming if that's happening for you.

BEGIN WITH A NONJUDGMENTAL OBSERVATION

As we get started, we're trying to take a step back from the way we've always assumed things should be done and that our child isn't currently on board with. We can start that process by making a nonjudgmental observation. This is a statement about the situation that does not place the blame on any of the people involved. It doesn't say to the child: "You have a problem that you need to fix so you can meet my standards," which creates distance and disconnection between us. It simply acknowledges: "There's an issue we're struggling with, and at least one of us isn't getting our needs met."

Many parents have a hard time making nonjudgmental observations because we've spent our entire lives judging others! They have a really hard time shifting from "Can you tell me what's going on for you *when you refuse to brush your teeth?*" to "I've noticed we've had a hard time with brushing your teeth. Can we talk about that?"

Starter scripts

Here are two starter scripts you can use to get the conversation going. (There are more of these to come in the book, and they're all collected on page 209.)

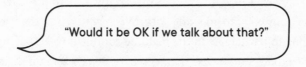

"I've noticed we're having a hard time . . ."

"It seems like we're struggling when . . ."

Then, once you've observed the situation, request permission to discuss it further.

"Would it be OK if we talk about that?"

We can't force a child to engage in this process; if they aren't a willing participant, then we're once again perpetuating our power over them, and they are less likely to want to engage in the future.

IS OUR WAY THE ONLY WAY?

As we're making our nonjudgmental observation, we should ask ourselves two questions:

What's the reason I feel like I "need" my child to do this (and do it in this way)?

Is it possible that I really *don't* need them to do this?

When we ask these two questions, we may find amazing possibilities.

What's the reason I "need" to do this?

As parents, we often assume we know what needs to be done, why it needs to be done, when it needs to be done (*right now!*), and how to do it. After all, we've been on the Earth for a while now, and we've figured out some routines that work pretty well, right? And if our child would just see things from our perspective, then they would know that what we're asking them to do is reasonable (and thus they should comply with our wishes).

Ask a hundred of your closest friends with young children how they navigate the bedtime routine, and you'll get a hundred different answers. There are a hundred different ways of doing any task! It simply isn't true that there's one "right" way to do it that we *must* get our child to go along with. We may find that they are quite willing to participate in the bedtime routine if we're paying attention to them so they feel connected, or if we warm up their pajamas in the dryer for a few minutes, or if we do bath time half as often. They might want to read stories in the living room instead of in bed, or under a blanket with a flashlight, or before going to the toilet one last time instead of after. We might find that a whole lot of these struggles disappear if we allow the child to play quietly in their room after story time rather than requiring them to stay in bed if they're not tired (an approach that's endorsed by sleep specialist Dr. Chris Winter). Yes, our child will end up in bed, but that doesn't mean that this process *must* follow the one path we've unilaterally decided is the right one.

What if we don't actually "need" to do this?

There are a few tasks that really do have to get done. If we work during the day, our child's preschool is too far away to walk to, and there's no bus, they really must get strapped into the car seat. A child's teeth aren't going to fall out if they miss brushing today, but if they miss brushing every day, then we're going to have painful and expensive problems. There are ideas coming for those challenges in Chapter 6.

If we think about it, though, there are a whole lot of other things we try to get our children to do that maybe we don't actually *need* to do. The table on the following page offers potential examples (and ways they're linked to White supremacy, patriarchy, and capitalism), and alternative ways we could handle the challenges.

WE TRY TO GET OUR CHILD TO	BECAUSE	INSTEAD, MAYBE WE COULD
Get dressed in certain clothes	We want them to conform to gender norms (patriarchy) or convey messages about our status (capitalism).	Choose from a limited selection of clothes they find comfortable.
Get dressed at all!	We've been trained that we should be presentable at all times (patriarchy).	Require minimal clothing (e.g., underwear only) when at home.
Eat certain foods	We're taught that there are "correct" foods to eat and less correct foods, and our ability as a parent can be measured by whether our child eats the right amount of "correct" foods (White supremacy, capitalism).	Make available a variety of foods appropriate to our culture (which may not fit White cultural norms).
Do routines (getting ready to leave the house, getting ready for bed) in a certain way	We assume that the things we've decided should happen must really happen, and in the order that we want them to happen (patriarchy).	Determine which elements of the routine we don't need to do at all, which we can shift to when we're better resourced (e.g., earlier in the day), and which we can do in different ways.
Say "please" and "thank you"	We want our children to confirm our position of power over them, and reflect our good parenting as they interact with others (patriarchy).	Model what we'd like our child to say ("You'd like some more milk, please?") while going to get the milk; say "please" and "thank you" to other people on their behalf.

WE TRY TO GET OUR CHILD TO	BECAUSE	INSTEAD, MAYBE WE COULD
Help with certain household chores (make their bed, put clothes away)	We want our children to do what those in positions of authority tell them (patriarchy), and be willing to work hard at things they don't like to do (capitalism).	Understand our true need (e.g., to feel a sense of collaboration with our child) and find ways they can help us that they enjoy.
Attend certain extracurricular activities	We think opportunities in life are limited and will be more available to our child if we've given them a "well-rounded" experience (capitalism).	Participate in fewer activities and consider activities the whole family enjoys.

When we look carefully, we may find that we're spending quite a lot of time on achievements and tasks that don't actually meet our needs, and we're doing them simply because it seems like we *should* do them—because that's what White supremacist, patriarchal, capitalist norms tell us to do. By letting go of some of these ideas, it's possible that we can create a whole lot more ease between us and our child.

And for the things that really do have to happen, the following chapters will guide you through a way to meet your needs *and* your child's needs: no rewards or punishments required!

CHAPTER 3

EMOTIONS AND REGULATION

How to Navigate Tantrums, Meltdowns, and Shutdowns

When our children are babies, we're completely focused on their needs. We remove things from their reach to keep them safe, we get up at all hours of the night to feed and comfort them, and we reorganize our lives around them.

Around the time they become mobile, a shift happens in us as parents. We start to say no to our child, and a kind of gap opens in our minds between what we think our child can do and what our child can actually do. This often happens when our child does something new once, and we think they should be able to do it *every time from then on.* The challenge for us is that we've forgotten what it was like to be a child, and we assume that our children think similarly to adults. If we told another adult fifty times "Don't touch that" or "Don't jump on the couch," we'd expect them to be able to remember, and to comply.

But our young children often can't remember or comply.

In 2016 the well-respected organization Zero to Three published the results of a parent survey that found a huge discrepancy between what parents think children can do at a specific age and what children can actually do.

SKILL	AGE AT WHICH PARENTS THINK CHILDREN HAVE THIS SKILL	APPROXIMATE AGE AT WHICH THIS SKILL IS ACTUALLY ATTAINED
Can share and take turns with other children	Between birth and six months (18 percent of parents think this) By age one or two (38 percent of parents think this)	Three to four years
Can control their emotions, such as not having a tantrum when frustrated	Before age one (24 percent of parents think this) Before age two (18 percent of parents think this)	Three and a half to four years
Can resist the desire to do something parents have forbidden	Before age three (56 percent of parents think this)	Three and a half to four years

SKILL	AGE AT WHICH PARENTS THINK CHILDREN HAVE THIS SKILL	APPROXIMATE AGE AT WHICH THIS SKILL IS ACTUALLY ATTAINED
Can remember a list of tasks and complete them	Before age two (36 percent of parents think this)	Around three years: remembers one to two tasks at a time. Up to around seven years: remembers five tasks at a time. Ability improved with visual reminders
Can name feelings and needs	No data is available from Zero to Three on parents' ideas of when children develop these skills	Varies by age and amount of time you've been practicing; appears on the early side around age three if the parent has been scaffolding this ability by hypothesizing aloud about the child's feelings and needs

This "expectations gap" creates a huge potential for difficulties between parents and children, as the parent asks the child to do a task they aren't yet developmentally capable of doing.

There's another challenge as well—one that is much more difficult to see because our (patriarchal) culture teaches us not to see it. The underlying issue is that our toddler is beginning to assert their needs, and because we spent our entire childhoods being told our needs weren't important, we don't know how to handle this. When we were young and we started to tell our parents our needs, they told us to be quiet and to do what we were told. (We'll dig into this further in Chapter 5.) For now, let's consider what's happening when our children are having tantrums, answering back, and refusing to cooperate.

After our child stops being a cute infant (when we meet their every need and ignore our own) and becomes a toddler, our culture tells us to stop meeting their needs and instead squash these as fast as possible, because we have no model for meeting two people's needs in a relationship.

Patriarchy says that one person must always be dominant: White people over everyone else, the male in a heterosexual partnership, the mother over the child. When a child has needs and knows that in our dominant position we won't meet those needs, they can't out-logic us. They can't argue their point. When we dominate over our children, the only tools they have to manage the big feelings that arise from this is to refuse. That's why they tantrum, answer back, and hit—acts that seem like defiance to us because they challenge our authority.

The angry words, tantrums, and hitting aren't pathological behaviors; it's that our children see that we're trying to exert control over them, and they're resisting—just as *we* used to resist our own parents doing this when we were children. We were trained to stop considering our own feelings and to prioritize our parents' feelings and comfort, which is why we have such a hard time with this today—because our child "acting out" reminds us of the ways we were punished for behaving in this way.

When we empathize with our children's struggles and look for ways to meet their needs *while also meeting ours*, we are likely to find that this difficult behavior diminishes rapidly. I'm not promising that if you use the Problem-Solving Approach then your child will never have another tantrum. There will still be instances when things just feel overwhelming and they can't stay regulated enough to communicate their needs, and the only thing they can do is cry and flail on the floor. But if your child is having tantrums about the same things over and over again, and these are *not* related to hunger, fatigue, or other basic bodily needs (which we should also try to meet when we can!), then learning to see and meet their needs is going to make a *dramatic* difference.

In the next few chapters, we'll break down all the components of our child's difficult behavior. We've actually already begun by approaching situations without judging them (and thus, by not punishing and rewarding). In this step, we need to know what to do about our child's big feelings, which may be quite triggering to us if we weren't allowed to express our feelings as children.

Patriarchal culture tells us that women and girls must never express "bad" feelings like sadness, frustration, and anger—we must be sponges for other people's feelings that are too painful for them to feel on their own. Boys mustn't express any feelings at all except anger, even when they desperately seek connection with others.

One parent I work with, Caroline, remembers not being able to express how she felt to her parents when she was a child. She remembers an incident when she and her younger brother were both little: she felt angry with him and pushed him, so he fell and hit his head and needed stitches; there was blood everywhere, and she felt both scared and incredibly sad. She didn't know how to communicate her big feelings and had no one to turn to who could understand or help her with them; when she tried to go to her parents with difficult feelings, they shut her out. It wasn't acceptable for a girl to feel anger toward her sibling, so her parents pretended it wasn't happening. Her mom would shut herself in her room and not allow Caroline to come in, no matter how upset Caroline was. She came to believe that her mother couldn't be with her because there was something wrong with Caroline herself, that she wasn't lovable enough—a feeling that has stayed with her for her whole life.

She learned to squash her difficult feelings to present a version of herself that would be acceptable to her parents, and now she does this with everyone else in her life too.

This longing to have our feelings acknowledged can result in far-reaching consequences. The anger, shame, and humiliation that we felt in childhood didn't go away; we just learned to cope with those feelings in more or less socially acceptable ways: excessive mothering (for women, leading to parental burnout); excessive working (for men, leading to "not enough time" to understand and communicate their feelings); emotional and physical violence toward women (from men); self-medication with drugs and alcohol (both). This is a gender binary based on patterns I often see in heterosexual relationships, although anyone can feel the consequences of not belonging and express these in a variety of ways.

EMPATHY IS KEY

When we first learn about respectful parenting, we're told that we must empathize with our child's struggles because this will help them to navigate difficult situations. So it can be really confusing when we empathize with our child's big feelings . . . and find that they cry more! It's not stopping the tantrum; it's making it worse! This begins to make sense in the context of mirroring: if you didn't experience this as a child and you're able to develop a relationship with a good therapist, they will likely mirror you, and then you may find that the experience of having another person show that they "get" your experience opens up the floodgates: you cry more from the relief of *finally* feeling understood.

MIRRORING

Mirroring involves (often unconsciously) copying another person's body language, speech, facial expression, and other nonverbal cues, as well as expressing verbally that we understand them. When a parent does this with a young child, the child learns that their feelings are acceptable to the parent and that the parent empathizes with their experience.

Parent Alex has a four-year-old who would hit, kick, throw toys, and threaten to hurt his parents ("I will punch you in the face if you don't get me the green bowl!") when things didn't go his way. Alex felt swept away in these moments with anger, frustration, and a sense of loss and failure. She felt a lot of stress to make it stop because her teenage babysitter also couldn't cope with it and was on the verge of quitting, and her partner thought it was time to start punishing their son by taking away toys and TV time.

When I coached Alex, we "slowed down time," as she described one of these interactions, which often happened when their one-on-one time was coming to an end as the two of them got ready to pick up his older sibling from school. We realized that she would usually respond to him saying "I don't *want* to go!" with a rationalization like: "But we have to go!" Alex still struggles with the pain of not having felt understood by her own mother when she was a child, which made it doubly difficult for her to acknowledge her son's feelings. More recently, Alex has been practicing having empathy for herself and her struggle in these difficult moments first, and then being present and empathizing with his feelings without trying to fix anything. She simply sat with him and told him she understood how hard it was to end their time alone and transition into time where he had to share her attention and connection with his sibling. She stopped telling herself that this was something she needed to fix and convincing him that they had to leave. She empathized that he didn't want their special time to end. She's noticed that he has far fewer and less intense meltdowns now, and that they last for shorter periods of time. Alex completely shifted from attempting to change her child's behavior to changing how *she* showed up in these interactions—which then enabled her son to respond from a place of being heard and understood. She used to describe their relationship as "disconnected" and says she would wake up each morning dreading the day with him. Now she sees that when she's consistent in her intention and her presence with him, each day gets a little better, which leads to fewer tantrums and an overall better relationship.

HOW TO EXPRESS EMPATHY

There's no one best way to express empathy; you'll need to experiment with these methods to see which resonate with your child. What's more important than the exact words you use is that you convey the impression that you are genuinely trying to use the four defining attributes of empathy. The good news is that we've already been practicing one of the four (being nonjudgmental) already!

THE FOUR DEFINING ATTRIBUTES OF EMPATHY

1 Seeing the world as others see it
2 Being nonjudgmental
3 Understanding another's feelings
4 Communicating your understanding

The following pages detail some of the ways that we might have been interacting with our child up to now that create a sense of disconnection between us . . . and ways we can start to create connection through empathy.

1. Seeing the world as others see it

When we fail to see the world as others see it, we often minimize and trivialize their struggles. This happens with our children and also with people who "aren't like us" out in the wider world; we become ethnocentric when we assume that our way of understanding the world is the *only* way of understanding it. Trying to see the world from our child's perspective is a crucial precursor to communicating empathy to our child, and it models the process for them so they will become practiced in seeing things from others' perspectives as well. Note that these are *not* necessarily things we might say to our child. Our child doesn't need or want to hear how we've been through similar struggles in our own lives; this is a tool to help *us* to understand the magnitude of our child's experiences.

THINGS WE MIGHT HAVE THOUGHT THAT SHOW WE DON'T SEE THE WORLD AS OUR CHILD SEES IT	THINGS WE MIGHT THINK TO SEE THE WORLD AS OUR CHILD SEES IT INSTEAD
"It's just a freaking spoon—why do I have to get up in the middle of my dinner *again* because they *just* decided they want the green spoon?"	"Having the green spoon every day helps them to feel a sense of order, and it's in the dishwasher. I know what it's like to feel discombobulated by things feeling out of order."
"Oh, for goodness' sake. All I'm asking them to do is brush their teeth. Don't they know there are children their age in other parts of the world who are responsible for an infant's safety? Why do they make such a big deal out of it?"	"Brushing teeth really isn't very interesting—I'm usually looking at my phone when I brush mine. And I only do it because I don't want to be in pain and spend thousands of dollars if I don't. But my child doesn't see that far ahead; they only see how unpleasant it is *now*."
"My child is so *lazy*. Don't they see how much work I do around the house? Unloading the dishwasher is hardly a *monumental* task."	"I've been feeling pretty disconnected from my child lately, and I wonder if they feel it too. Perhaps they're refusing to help because they're trying to say they don't feel like they're valued in our family right now."

2. Being nonjudgmental

When we're judgmental, we create a massive disconnection between ourselves and the other person because nobody likes to be judged—even our child!

JUDGMENTAL THINGS WE MIGHT HAVE SAID TO OUR CHILD	NONJUDGMENTAL THINGS WE COULD SAY INSTEAD
"You hit your head on the table again, huh? I've told you a hundred times that if you run around in the kitchen, you're probably going to get hurt."	"Did you hit your head?" [Child]: "Yes." "Does it hurt, or did it surprise you?"
"If you would just cooperate, you could be in and out of the shower in two minutes, and I wouldn't get soap in your eyes."	"It seems like showering has been difficult for us lately, especially when I wash your hair. Can you tell me how you feel when I'm washing your hair?"
"Why are you sad? You're going to your friend's house as soon as you get dressed, and you love it there!"	"It seems like you're having a hard time this morning, huh? Would you like to tell me about it?"

3. Understanding another's feelings, and 4. communicating your understanding

When we show that we don't understand what our child is feeling, they shut down—and when we show we're not even *trying* to understand, they'll refuse to engage in these kinds of conversations in the future. When we communicate that we're at least trying to understand, our child is more likely to want to continue the conversation with us.

THINGS WE MIGHT HAVE SAID TO OUR CHILD THAT SHOW THEM THAT WE DON'T UNDERSTAND THEIR FEELINGS ABOUT SOMETHING THAT'S IMPORTANT TO THEM	THINGS WE COULD SAY TO SHOW OUR CHILD THAT WE UNDERSTAND THEIR FEELINGS ABOUT SOMETHING THAT'S IMPORTANT TO THEM
"Why are you making such a fuss? It's just a broken cracker!"	"I can see you're really upset that the cracker broke. Do you wish it could be whole again?"
"You're OK! You're OK! You're not hurt!"	"Oh, it really surprised you when you fell, huh?"
"I know it hurt your feelings when Sam said that, but they didn't mean it. You just have to ignore them."	"How did you feel when Sam said that to you?" [Child]: "I didn't like it. I hate them!" "Oh, I hear you. It sounds like you feel really hurt, is that right?"

HOW DO I KNOW WHAT MY CHILD IS FEELING?

When we're just getting started with this kind of work, it can
be very difficult to understand our child's—and even our own!—
feelings. Consulting a list, like the List of Feelings starting on
page 206, may help you get started. We actually may find that we
regularly experience a fairly small set of feelings. I think of it like
eating a cupcake: when we're not sure what we (or our child) is
feeling, we can eat the cherry on top by considering the top three
to five feelings that are the usual suspects first. Then perhaps the
next three to five after that (lick off the frosting). And if nothing fits,
then consider other possibilities (taste the cake).

Here's how I see feelings showing up in me and in my daughter
when things aren't going well:

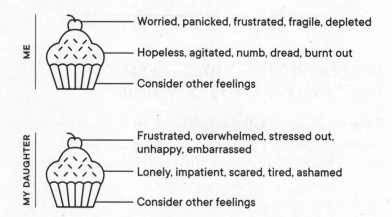

If none of the usual suspects seem to fit, then I look to a broader
set of feelings (the cupcake)—but having the short list to start
with is especially helpful when either of us is feeling dysregulated
because it helps us to understand each other more quickly. You
may want to create a feelings cupcake for yourself and another for

your child so you can refer back to it when you need to. There's a template to help you on page 210.

Starter scripts

Here are some starter scripts to help you with this part of the conversation:

> "Could you share how you were feeling when that happened?"
>
> "What was going on for you when that happened?"
>
> "Could you tell me how you feel about ... ?"
>
> "I'm wondering if you're feeling ... ?"
>
> "I'm feeling ... right now."

WHAT SHOULD I DO IF MY CHILD CAN'T OR WON'T EXPRESS FEELINGS IN WORDS?

Some parents become discouraged at this point in the process because their child can't or won't use feelings words, so they don't see how this method can 'work.' Here are two ideas that can help:

1   Say what you see: "I see that you're jumping around the room and you have a big smile—you seem really excited!" or "Your forehead is crinkled and your lips are pulled together tight like this [demonstrate] and you're standing with your elbows out, and I'm wondering if you're feeling angry?"

2   Develop an energy-meter that relates the child's experience to a topic of their interest. Dr. Jacquelyn Fede made a dinosaur

energy-meter with "T. Rex on a Tear" as the top energy level; her grandmother used to describe energy levels to her using Winnie-the-Pooh characters ("You're looking a little Tigger"). You can draw this on a sheet of paper so you and your child can both refer to the pictures even if your child doesn't speak.

HOLD UP!

One thing I see a lot of parents do when they're new to the Problem-Solving Approach is jump right from empathizing to solutions. Please don't do this!

Underneath feelings are needs, and it's critical that we understand those needs before we jump to potential solutions—otherwise, the solutions we land on probably aren't going to meet someone's (most likely our child's) needs. This looks like:

Parent: "You feel frustrated right before you hit your sibling? (*Feeling*) OK! How about you hit a pillow instead?" (*Solution*)

Child: "OK."

The next day, the child feels frustrated, but their need for connection with their parent still hasn't been met, so they hit their sibling again. Then the parent feels frustrated because this method "doesn't work." The child may not be able to say why the solution doesn't work for them because they don't have language to understand their needs yet; all they know is that they can't or don't want to use the solution. Problem solving how to change a child's behavior doesn't work, because nobody likes being told to change their behavior

Try to read at least Chapter 4 before you jump into problem-solving mode with your child.

EXERCISE

- Are you able to identify your feelings as you move through your day? How about when you're having a difficult interaction with your child? Consult the List of Feelings starting on page 206 if that would be helpful. You may find you experience five to ten feelings most regularly. Write these on your feelings cupcake template on page 210, or download a full-sized version from https://www.YourParentingMojo.com/BookBonuses.

- Practice identifying your feelings: set a timer to go off five to ten times during the day, or if you do something regularly during the day (pray, drink tea, pee), make a point to check in and see how you're feeling before, after, or while doing these things. Use the feelings list if it helps.

- When you're having a difficult interaction with your child, try to identify your feelings. If it's too hard in the moment, do it after the fact. If you observe anger, try to see what's underneath that feeling, as anger almost always covers something we don't want others to see (fear, shame, etc.).

- The next time your child is expressing big feelings, try simply being present with what comes up for you. If you can get beyond the idea that your job is to make the big feelings stop at all costs, does something shift? Can you see that your child is trying to communicate something to you? When you're calm again, can you try to understand what that thing is?

CHAPTER 4:

CHILDREN'S RESISTANCE

A Gift That Shows Us Their Needs

Up to this point in your child's life, you might have assumed that your problem was that your child *won't listen to you*, which they indicate by not doing what you ask or tell them to do. After all, you're the parent and you need to get them to do certain things (get ready for day care/school, brush their teeth, go to bed), right? You remind them twenty times in a louder voice and with more frustration each time so, of course, the problem is that they need to listen better— and then do what you ask or tell them to do.

It turns out that there are a whole host of reasons why children don't listen to us (and don't do what we ask). Here are some examples:

- The child doesn't want to stop what they're doing. (How often do *you* want to stop in the middle of something you're enjoying?)

- The child didn't hear you. (This is more common than you might think, especially if you aren't making eye contact.)

- The child doesn't understand time well enough to know how much they have left before a transition will happen.

- The child can't remember all the things you've asked them to do. (Breaking tasks down into more manageable chunks can help.)

- The child feels disconnected from you and is resisting as a way of indicating this. (Try some more empathetic communication; see Chapter 3.)

- The child has been conditioned to wait until you yell.

- The child feels judged by the way you're asking them to do the task.

- The child wants more autonomy over things that happen in their lives—they want a say in what happens, and how it happens.

- The child doesn't want to do the task, for reasons you may not fully understand. (This is the focus of this chapter!)

When our child isn't doing what we want them to do, we very rarely stop to ask *why* the child isn't cooperating. In a patriarchal culture, it isn't important that we understand why; what's important is our ability to get our child to do what we want. As we work to break down patriarchal power structures, we're going to identify the needs underlying our child's resistance—and our own resistance as well!

The diagram on the next page shows how conflict typically shows up in families who have been heavily impacted by Eurocentric culture.

FAMILY CONFLICT IN A SOCIETY DOMINATED BY WHITE SUPREMACY, PATRIARCHY, AND CAPITALISM

PROBLEM: CHILD REFUSES TO BRUSH TEETH

Parent draws on what they were taught when they were a child.

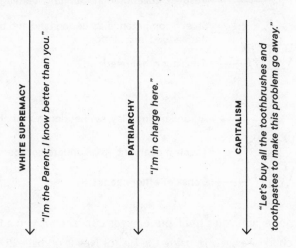

WHITE SUPREMACY
"I'm the Parent; I know better than you."

PATRIARCHY
"I'm in charge here."

CAPITALISM
"Let's buy all the toothbrushes and toothpastes to make this problem go away."

Parent says: "Brush your teeth!"

Parent does: Buys everything that might help

Child says: "No! I don't want to brush teeth!"

Power struggle

Stalemate

Rewards, punishments,
coercion to get the job done

ALL PEOPLE HAVE NEEDS

The idea of needs is drawn from Non-Violent Communication, which was pioneered by Marshall Rosenberg. Just as with feelings, I find it really helpful to have a list of my and my child's three to five most common needs (our "needs cupcake") to reduce the amount of effort it takes to figure out why we're having a hard time:

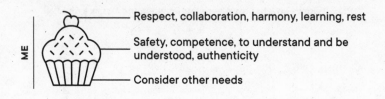

ME — Respect, collaboration, harmony, learning, rest

Safety, competence, to understand and be understood, authenticity

Consider other needs

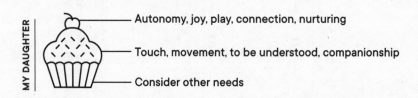

MY DAUGHTER — Autonomy, joy, play, connection, nurturing

Touch, movement, to be understood, companionship

Consider other needs

Once again, you can fill out a needs cupcake for you and your child on page 211, using the List of Needs on page 208 if necessary—this should help you to understand much more quickly what might be happening when your child is resisting you.

The more you see your child resisting you in *a lot* of different areas, the more you should look for needs outside of specific difficult situations and instead look at your relationship more generally. Most commonly I see this happening when a child's need for connection and/or autonomy isn't being met. For connection, try repeated, predictable 1:1 play that the child gets to direct even for just 10 minutes, every day. For autonomy, try relaxing as many limits as possible. You may well find that once these needs are met, your child stops fighting you in a lot of different situations.

NEEDS VERSUS STRATEGIES (AND WANTS)

I'm going to shift for a moment to look at needs in adults, because I think that's more intuitive for parents.

Sometimes we use ineffective strategies to meet our needs. When I pick a fight with my husband because he didn't unload the dishwasher (again), my need isn't about the dishwasher—it's about needing collaboration and teamwork, and I'm using an unskillful strategy (trying to get him to unload the dishwasher) to meet those needs. The key ideas here are:

- All people have needs.

- We often try to use unskillful strategies to meet our needs.

- We often get attached to our strategies (and when our children do this, we call them "wants").

- We can never be sure we understand another person's needs until they tell us. (Although we can hypothesize about their needs, and with a young child, we can often do this fairly accurately.)

- There are always multiple strategies we can use to meet a need, and it's usually possible to meet both people's needs in an interaction.

Let's consider each of these ideas in the context of my example with the dishwasher:

- You have needs—for things like rest, self-care, connection with others, autonomy, intellectual stimulation, and so on. Your parenting partner has needs too—likely some are different than yours. Your child has needs as well. We acknowledged those needs and tried to meet them when they were a baby, but as soon as they became a toddler, our culture told us that they must be socialized: which means teaching them that their needs aren't important and our *strategies* should come first. We don't know how to look for our underlying needs—or theirs—and how we can meet both.

- As children, we went through a process of being socialized to ignore our needs, which is the main reason we use unskillful strategies. Remember parent Stephanie, who told me that, prior to working with me, she "didn't even know what it meant to have a need"? Just think about the gravity of that statement. This parent's needs had been ignored and overridden so often in childhood that she didn't even know that she had needs, never mind how to go about meeting them. Is it any wonder that we insist that the strategy we've chosen is the only one that will work, not realizing that there are myriad other ways we could get our needs met? And is it any wonder that we feel so incredibly threatened when our child asserts their needs? Not understanding needs makes it more difficult to imagine why other people might be doing the things we find mystifying, confusing, and irritating, which means we're likely to misattribute their motives based on our previous experience. Working to understand people's needs helps us to view them as whole, complex beings whose needs are just as important as our own.

- We can hypothesize about another person's needs (and when we're working with young children who can't communicate verbally with us yet, we'll be doing a lot of this), although we can never really know what their needs are until they tell us. But even if we guess wrong, the process of considering that the other person might have a need that hadn't occurred to us can be really helpful. When I'm unloading the dishwasher again, my overactive left brain (which likes to make up stories to make sense of my experiences that are only tangentially connected to reality) is saying: *My partner is lazy. He doesn't see how hard I work. He doesn't care about how much I do around the house, and he isn't interested in splitting the work equally.* When I ask myself: *Is it possible that what I believe isn't true?* I can consider another option: that perhaps he has a need for a slow start in the morning. It doesn't especially matter if I'm right: just by considering another reason for the behavior I'm seeing, I'm getting out of a judgmental mindset and into a curious one so I can work to understand his needs.

- The awesome part about needs is that there are always many, many ways to meet them. If I tell my partner that I'm missing a sense of collaboration and teamwork in our relationship, I will most likely find that he is quite willing to help me meet that need. Perhaps he will unload the dishwasher . . . sometime before lunch. Or take on other tasks around the house. Or help me get more working time by taking our daughter out for the day. Or just acknowledge the work I'm doing. Each of these strategies could help meet my need for collaboration—and I might also find that my partner has needs that aren't being met that I could help him to meet as well.

Now let's apply these ideas to our relationship with our children. When our children express their needs (often in very unskillful ways: "I don't *want* to brush my teeth"; "I want to keep playing!"; or just "No!") and we try to override their needs, the only option they have is to dig in, which is when we see tantrums, disobedience, and defiance.

I'm not saying that we should 100 percent acquiesce to everything our child wants—far from it. Sometimes we ask children to do things that they don't want to do but that we, with our fully developed brains and decades of experience, know really is in their best interest. Things like taking medication, undergoing medical procedures, and even brushing their teeth. (Although this last one can fall into a gray area depending on your family's dental history. Some children won't experience any ill effects from brushing every couple of days; others are headed for fillings even after brushing twice a day.) We're not offering them the option to not do things that are critical for their health and well-being—although we may still be able to meet more of their needs related to these activities than we have been doing.

What I am suggesting is that:

- The number of things that are critical to their health and well-being that we ask them to do are fairly few.

- Most of the things we ask them to do are really for our convenience, and as we discussed earlier, perhaps a number of them don't even need to be done.

- For those that still need to be done, there are likely ways to do them that meet our child's needs.

Having a set bedtime is a prime example of something that parents feel is critical to the child's well-being that may not really be such big deal. However much sleep our child is getting, many of us think they should be getting more. The National Sleep Foundation recommends that toddlers aged one to two years get eleven to fourteen hours of sleep, but acknowledges that there are likely some who need less and others who need more—perhaps nine hours on the low end and sixteen hours on the high end. That's a difference of seven hours! The same goes for preschoolers aged three to five years, with ten to thirteen hours recommended and a possible range of eight to fourteen hours: a difference of six hours.

Very often, when we're trying to get a child into bed in the evening, it isn't only because we're concerned about our child's need for rest—it's because we're trying to meet our *own* need for rest, self-care, and/or accomplishment (work). We're asking our child to do something that doesn't meet their needs (which might include fun/joy, connection with us, competence through finishing a project, etc.—as well as the fact that they might not even be tired) so that we can meet our needs.

What if there was a way to meet both people's needs? What we're moving toward trying to do is making sure your children are getting the sleep they need without forcing them to lie in bed when they aren't tired. What if your child could continue whatever project they were working on or look at books or play quietly in their room after a certain time each night? Wouldn't that allow them to meet their needs and also free up time for us to meet our needs?

This approach does rely on us believing that our children can listen to their own bodies and understand their own needs, which our culture says isn't really possible. That's why we constantly second-guess them:

"Are you sure you've had enough? How about just one more bite?"

"I don't care if you say you're not cold; put a jacket on."

"Go try to pee before we leave the house, even if you don't need to go."

"It doesn't matter if you're not tired; it's bedtime."

Every person is the expert on their own body, but by shutting down their self-advocacy, we're actively training our children to ignore what they know to be true about their bodies. The same thing happened to us when we were children, and is perpetuated by our culture even today. I often begin group coaching calls with a few moments of mindfulness practice, and afterward we do a check-in to see what came up for people. Pretty often, someone will say something like: "I had no idea how hungry I was, so I'm getting a snack," or "I just realized I have a headache, and I think I've had it for most of the day." The Protestant work ethic that's embedded in many Eurocentric cultures trains us to override our needs, to push on and finish the job no matter what. We're also taught that our bodies aren't a useful source of information: we are taught that all worthwhile information processing happens within the brain, which then "gives the orders" to our body. If we don't look at our bodies as a valuable source of information, then why would we pay attention to cues like hunger or a headache? We're just going to power on through anyway. So when our children do express their needs, we implicitly tell them: "Your needs don't matter; what matters is that you comply with my wishes." Parenting coach Hannah Olavarria of Upbringing once said on a coaching call we were leading together: "We have the power in the parent-child relationship, but the child has all the awareness." Our task is to understand what they're aware of that we aren't, and to share the power in a way that meets everyone's needs. When we can do this, we're likely to find the child is much more willing to collaborate with us—and also learns invaluable lessons about paying attention to their bodies, consent, and taking actions that are aligned with their values—lessons that are much better learned through relationships and modeling than through trying to instruct the child.

RESISTANCE IS THE STRUGGLE AGAINST OUR NEEDS NOT BEING MET

When we try to strong-arm our children into ignoring their needs, they resist! Of course they resist! What we're trying to get them to do goes against every fiber of their being! They say no; they stall and drag their feet; they throw tantrums.

This can be incredibly difficult for parents to cope with, because when we were children and tried to resist our parents we were likely shamed, humiliated, and punished—even if only in subtle ways, like a certain disapproving look or a cooling of affection. Now when our child tries to assert their needs, it triggers all of that old hurt. If we were very young when it happened, before we have conscious memories of the event, we might not even know why we feel triggered.

But I work with plenty of parents who do remember: they remember their parent freaking out when they talked back or expressed any feeling other than happiness and gratitude. And very often, it's exactly these same situations that become triggering for them: their child expresses a need, and the parent loses it. Masako, whose child didn't want to take a bath, remembers that her mother was very hard on herself whenever she made a mistake or was careless. She would curse in French (as Japanese doesn't have strong curse words that women are permitted to use), and because she was from an upper-class family and normally very soft-spoken, the cursing really stood out to Masako. Even if Masako's dad was totally fine with whatever dinner was served, her mom would apologize profusely if a dish didn't come out perfectly. Masako also remembers visiting family when she was about five and spilling milk on her sweater. Her uncle quickly wiped the spill away and said, "Let's keep your mom from finding out or she'll get upset." Hiding things from her mom became a theme: not long afterward, Masako got a blistering second-degree burn from a kerosene stove at a friend's house, and Masako hid this from her mother because she knew her mother would be upset by her carelessness. Even though Masako's mom rarely directly reprimanded her, Masako still internalized these ideas. Because she's been working on more awareness of her reactions, Masako has realized she will gasp as a sign of her own overwhelm (rather than yell at her own child). She's working on exhaling slowly to help manage her reaction, but she often still finds she needs to leave the room for a minute to calm down. Once again, even though she has never directly reprimanded her son for accidents, at three years old, he gets upset if he spills something—he has sensed the disruption in the connection between the two of them when these events happen.

THE DENIAL OF NEEDS LEADS TO PAIN

Hopefully it's clear that just getting our child to change their behavior to comply with our wishes isn't a desirable goal. Through the judgments that come with rewards and punishments, through ignoring their feelings, through denying their needs until they begin to forget what their needs are and how to identify them, we create a deep disconnection between us and our child. They learn that we cannot or will not accept them as their genuine selves. If they're not strong enough to be defiant, they split off the part of themselves that is genuine and authentic and present only a sanitized version to their parent. They could become a model student, getting straight As, doing all the extracurriculars, and volunteering, and it may seem like everything is under control—until, at some point, it isn't. They might actively rebel against you (arguing, shutting down), or look for ways to numb their emotional pain (such as through alcohol or drugs), or seek out anyone who will accept them (even those who aren't true friends or positive influences). For those who are especially successful at making the split, they might get all the way through college and into a financially successful career, putting one foot in front of the other each day, making decisions based on the fact that everyone else is doing the same thing, just to make you happy. Then they wake up one day in midlife wondering what the heck they're doing and how they got there.

The key to avoiding this split is to see our children for who they really are, and to see their needs as an expression of this, and to do what we can to meet those needs. What we're likely to find when we do this is that far from devolving into chaos, our family instead becomes a team where our children are invested in collaborating and cooperating with us. Even when we can't meet their needs (e.g., because they *must* have a medical procedure), they're much more likely to work with us because they know that we'll do everything we can to meet their needs the vast majority of the time.

Masako has used the Problem-Solving Conversations with her son starting when he was pretty young—about two and a half. Even if they didn't get to work the process all the way through, she found that she gained a lot by trying to be open and curious and guess at what he was feeling and needing. Sometimes they didn't even discuss any potential solutions to the problem they were trying to solve, but her son seemed to sense that she was trying to understand and work with him, which improved the situation—and now that he's older and they both have more practice, they're better able to identify each other's needs.

LEARNING TO HEAR WHAT "NO" REALLY MEANS

Because many of us were raised in families where we weren't allowed to say "no," when our child says "no" to us, we experience an almost unbearable rejection.

Instead of hearing the "no" as a rejection, we can learn to translate its meaning to: "That suggestion/idea/request doesn't meet my needs right now." Our children most often say "no" because resistance is the only tool they have to say that their need isn't being met. They don't yet have the vocabulary to explain it in a logical way (and we would out-argue them anyway), so they use their best available option. When we can see it's not that our child is refusing to get in the bath/use the potty/go to bed but, instead, they're saying that "this doesn't meet my need right now," we can work with them to understand why they're responding this way and how we can help them. As adrienne maree brown says, "Your clear 'no' makes way for your 'yes.' Being able to say what we don't want allows us to clear the path." Your child isn't rejecting you or refusing to cooperate. They're inviting you to collaborate on finding a path that works for both of you.

Non-Violent Communication practitioner Dr. Miki Kashtan writes that we try to train children to say: "Can I . . . ?" to ask our permission, acknowledging our full power. If they go into a teenage rebellion, they're more likely to say: "I'm going to . . ." (with the implied ending: "because you can't stop me"). In our family, both my daughter and I say things to each other like: "I'm going to . . . , OK?" or "I'm thinking of . . . ; what do you think?" This is a simple shift in intention, and such a challenge to top-down, power-based patriarchal models of parenting. It shows we care about our child's needs just as much as we care about our own!

The facing page illustrates a new way of seeing these kinds of conversations in our families.

HEALING-BASED APPROACH
TO FAMILY CONFLICT

Parent observes nonjudgmentally: "We've been having a hard time brushing teeth. Can we talk about that?"

UNDERSTAND <u>CHILD'S FEELINGS</u>	Bored, afraid, angry
UNDERSTAND <u>PARENT'S FEELINGS</u>	Tired, frustrated
UNDERSTAND <u>CHILD'S NEEDS</u>	Play/joy, ease, comfort, autonomy
UNDERSTAND <u>PARENT'S NEEDS</u>	Collaboration, protection of child's health, ease
POTENTIAL SOLUTIONS (propose each as a request. The solution that "works" is the one that addresses both the parent's and the child's needs)	• Play games while brushing • Brush more gently • Child chooses whether to brush teeth before or after stories • Child chooses toothbrush/ toothpaste • Watch a toothbrushing app while brushing • Parent with preferred brushing style helps • Child chooses to brush wrapped in fluffy blanket in front of heater
RESULTS	• Teeth brushed • Relationship strengthened • Power shared • Minimal purchases of additional equipment to address the problem

HOW TO IDENTIFY A CHILD'S NEEDS

Many parents I work with initially have a hard time identifying their child's needs. After all, how could we *possibly* know why our child is refusing to cooperate with us?

Most children are expressing one of a very few needs most of the time:

- Connection (often with us)

- Empathy (to know that we are trying to see things from their perspective)

- Safety (mostly emotional safety)

- Comfort (mostly physical, including heat/cold, softness/smoothness, and physical location of the body)

- Respect (to know that we consider their needs with the same care as our own)

- Play (including joy and fun)

- Integrity (to be able to act in alignment with their needs, rather than prioritizing our needs)

- Autonomy (to be able to make decisions about things that impact their life)

Refer to the List of Needs on page 208 to create your own needs cupcake (see page 211) and one for your child as well. Then when your child seems dysregulated (which they will show through resisting, tantrums, hitting, etc.) because they have a need that isn't being met, you can look at the cherry of most-common needs on their cupcake to try to figure out what's going on. Perhaps their sibling has been poking at them all morning (need for safety). Or you've been apart a lot more than usual recently (need for connection). Or they were really enjoying jumping around outside and didn't want to come inside (need for joy and movement).

You don't have to guess 100 percent correctly the first time; just give it a try and get started. Parent Lulu did this during a rough evening with her son. He requested a "special" bath where all the toys were dumped in the tub, and she gave him the option of that or extra time to play outside. He chose to play outside, but when it was bedtime, he had a meltdown because he wanted his special bath.

While it can be challenging to identify needs in the middle of a difficult situation, Lulu gave it a try: she guessed at his need. "Do you need to play?" Pause. No response. "Do you need more movement?" Pause. No response. "Do you need to be having fun right now?" Pause.

He responded: "I need to feel caring."

Lulu had no idea that "special bath" made her son feel cared for. This opened up the door to discuss other options to help him feel loved, and they found one that worked for them both—a long hug and Lulu washing him in the shower instead of him doing it himself. Their evening ended in closeness and connection, instead of tears and frustration at bedtime.

Lulu was new to this method at the time and took a big chance by trying to do it in a dysregulated moment. Many children who are new to the Problem-Solving Approach won't be able to identify and share their needs when they're already having a meltdown. If this happens, just get through the situation as best you can, with copious amounts of empathy, and make a plan to come back to a conversation about it when everyone's a lot more regulated (so, not right after the meltdown—you'll often need to wait several hours and maybe until the next day). When you're both ready, open up the conversation with a nonjudgmental observation. Then you can look at: "What is my child's need?" and "Am I willing to hold my child's need with as much care as my own, and consider unconventional strategies to meet both of our needs?"

In the next chapter, we'll look at *your* needs, and then how to meet your child's needs and yours together.

EXERCISE

- Think of a time when your parent or caregiver disciplined you when you were young. What was the infraction you committed? (This is the behavior that your parent was reacting to.) What need of yours were you meeting by committing the infraction? Can you imagine what need your parent might have had in that moment? What could they have done differently that would have helped you to meet your need in that moment?

- Are you able to identify your needs on a regular basis? How about when you are having a difficult interaction with your child? Consult the List of Needs on page 208 if that would be helpful. Write the top five to ten needs on your needs cupcake template on page 211. There's a full-page downloadable version available at https://www. YourParentingMojo.com/BookBonuses.

- Bring to mind an interaction in which your child resisted or refused your request. Using the List of Needs on page 208, can you hypothesize what need your child was trying to meet in this situation? Try to identify at least ten ways your child's need could have been met. Don't worry for right now about whether you would have found these strategies acceptable at the time—just focus on generating a long list to really get the sense that there are many ways to meet a need.

CHAPTER 5:

MEETING PARENTS' NEEDS

(Sometimes with Boundaries)

By this point, you might be thinking: *OK, that's great; I'm convinced that my child has needs, and I'm going to try to identify these and meet them when I can. But what about my needs?*

I'm so glad you asked! These are absolutely important too. In fact, if we're only focused on our child's needs, we're missing a huge piece of the picture.

WHY WE HAVE TROUBLE IDENTIFYING OUR NEEDS

Most of our parents were doing the best they could to raise us using limited information and navigating their own traumas at the same time—so they weren't able to see or meet our needs.

Most likely, our parents didn't meet our needs for one of three reasons:

- **They didn't see our needs.** Maybe they weren't around much or they were emotionally checked out as they dealt with their own challenges. If one of our siblings was often sick, our parent might not have been physically available to us. Our culture tells us to deny children's understandings of their own bodies, so we tell them to clean their plates (disregarding their signals of hunger/satiety), to put jackets on even when they aren't cold, to use the bathroom even when they don't need to, etc. This means that we aren't in the habit of even considering that children have needs when they refuse to do what we ask.

- **They considered and then disregarded our needs.** Sometimes our parents saw our needs but didn't think they should be met. In her book *The Drama of the Gifted Child*, Swiss psychologist Dr. Alice Miller tells a story of seeing two parents and a preschooler getting ice cream (for the parents but not for the child). The child desperately wanted the joyful experience of eating a delicious food, but the parents denied him repeatedly and then teased him about it.

- **They wanted to break our spirit.** Sometimes parents will have an explicit aim to "break" their child's spirit, particularly if the child has a trait or quality that is perceived to be socially undesirable in that family's community (e.g., introversion, dependence in male-identifying children, loudness in female-identifying children). Our parents might have seen us as defiant and wanted us to calm down, to stop asserting our needs, or to prioritize their comfort over our own.

The consequences of having had our needs ignored or overridden for so long are profound. We might see this on a regular basis when we snap at our child for doing something age appropriate and can't figure out why *this tiny thing* sends us over the edge—it's because we don't know how to identify our needs on a regular basis, and by the end of the day, we've had our needs ignored or overridden so many times that even one more request to meet someone else's needs feels utterly overwhelming.

I met parent Kelly when she reached out to me asking me to do a podcast episode discussing the parental burnout she was experiencing, and we ended up interviewing Dr. Moïra Mikolajczak—one of the world's leading researchers on this topic—together. More recently, Kelly learned that her grandmother had been very critical of her mother as a young child, so Kelly's mom vowed to be positive and always praise Kelly's behavior. But this ended up backfiring: Kelly learned quickly to be wary of this praise and to search for clues about whether her mom was truly excited about her achievements, rather than tuning into her own feelings about how she was doing. Kelly's mom wasn't responding to the needs of the child she had in front of her; she was parenting in reaction to her own unresolved hurt. Kelly couldn't identify her own needs as a child because she was so focused on trying to understand her mom's well-intentioned but confusing reactions to her behavior. Now, as an adult, Kelly often feels responsible for how others are feeling, and even sees that protecting her mom's feelings drove a wedge between Kelly and her husband. Kelly realized while taking my Taming Your Triggers workshop that the pattern her mom had established was repeating itself with her daughter, and she is now working to change this.

BODY-BRAIN SEPARATION OBSCURES OUR NEEDS

Separating our bodies and our brains is by now deeply ingrained in Eurocentric cultures. The ancient Greeks saw intellect as being superior to physical athleticism, and Christianity adopted this attitude. The brain is physically higher and is associated with light, purity, and heaven, while the body is physically lower and connected to misfortune, breaking down, and hell—and similar ideas show up in many other religions as well.

Philosopher René Descartes built on this idea by describing the body and brain as separate, and this "Cartesian split" has defined how we see the brain in the four hundred years since. The brain produces all the rational ideas that keep the systems running, and the body just takes the orders and does what it's told. The brain is presumed to perceive everything accurately and can make rational decisions; any information coming from the body is, at best, irrelevant and, at worst, interferes with our ability to make a rational decision.

BEGINNING TO UNDERSTAND *OUR* NEEDS

It isn't easy to do things differently when we've spent decades laying down these old tracks. It's much easier to just keep doing things the same way we've always done them because our brains learned these tools to keep us safe. Kelly's brain learned when she was a child: *You'd better pay attention to how other people are feeling: when they're really happy, you can be happy.* So initially, when her daughter started testing limits, Kelly showed her disappointment because she thought this would make her daughter want to change her behavior. Now Kelly is learning two very important skills. The first of these is understanding what she needs in the already difficult moments.

Covering her ears with her hands is a red flag indicating that she's overwhelmed by the noise in the house and needs a few minutes to reset by breathing slowly and deeply, stretching, listening to quiet music, or even having a good cry.

The second important skill is knowing what to do with the information you find in your body on a regular basis, which very often signals our needs much earlier than when we're in full-on red-flag territory. Kelly calls this the orange zone, and notices sensations like a shiver in her chest and stomach, shallow breathing, feeling easily distracted, eating faster, not being able to sit still, and feeling irritated at little things like hooking her pants pocket on a drawer or her daughter asking "why?" again. When we can learn to pay attention to these kinds of signals much earlier on in the process of a disagreement with another person, we can use that information to understand that we have an unmet need, and then communicate that need to them and ask for their help in meeting it.

It's often easiest to start understanding this after a need hasn't been met. Your child does something that makes you snap. As soon as possible after the event, after you're reregulated, try to remember what happened in the minutes and hours leading up to it. What sensations did you feel in your body? What did you notice right before you snapped? And what had been building throughout the day? Very often our bodies will try to send us lots of little signals, and we ignore them. Your child wants the blue cup instead of the red one, and you've already sat down to breakfast. You get the blue cup, but you feel a little something—perhaps a knot in your shoulders, a lump in your throat, or clenching in your stomach. Your child refuses to get dressed, and your temperature rises, but you manage to keep a lid on it. Ten more events like this happen throughout the day, and you keep disregarding your needs and try to give your child what they want. What was your body telling you each time?

Here are some of the wide variety of sensations that parents I work with experience in the build-up to difficult moments:

- Your heart beating more quickly

- A sensation of blood rushing to your head

- The hair on your arms standing on end

- A heavy feeling in your chest

- A tense jaw or clenched teeth

- Your skin starting to feel like it's vibrating and you need to escape it

- A tightness in your throat, chest, or shoulders

- A fluttery feeling in your chest

- Holding your breath

- A sense of nausea

- A headache

These are signs that you are becoming *dysregulated*: that you are finding it difficult to regulate your feelings, and you're in danger of reacting to your child in a way that isn't aligned with your values. Now when Kelly finds herself in the slightly dysregulated orange zone, she realizes it's often because of the overwhelm she feels as a result of taking on too many tasks herself. She's afraid to ask for help because it might cause the other person to think less of her (which is what created her burnout in the first place). She has begun a practice of self-talk, where she has conversations with herself: *What am I asking from this person? Is that reasonable? Was the person able to say no?* Kelly used to take on all the responsibility for both people's feelings in an attempt to protect the other person from having to say no to her. Now she has learned that as long as the person has a chance to say no, she can respect their choice to do something for her and accept and enjoy the favor. She has effectively divided the responsibilities of the interaction so each person navigates their own feelings, which prevents her from having to manage everyone's feelings. This mostly keeps her out of the red zone.

Parents often report that they have a need for *control* (which is ultimately what Kelly was trying to do: control all aspects of an interaction), but this tends to mask other underlying needs. When it seems like you have a "need" for control, consider what other feelings and needs might be underneath that—very often, we feel a fear of some kind: that our child will *never* learn a critical skill, that someone will judge us, that we won't look like we have it all together. Or perhaps we feel a sense of shame. And we all have needs for safety and security.

The basic categories of needs (and some common needs that parents have within those categories) are:

- **Connection:** Acceptance, appreciation, community, empathy, love, to understand and be understood

- **Physical well-being:** Air, comfort, food, movement/exercise, rest/sleep, water

- **Safety:** Consistency, physical and emotional safety

- **Honesty:** Authenticity, integrity

- **Relaxation:** Humor, joy, mental space

- **Peace:** Beauty, ease, harmony, order, respect

- **Autonomy:** Choice, freedom, independence, spontaneity

- **Meaning:** Challenge, competence, creativity, growth, learning, self-expression, to have a sense of purpose

You will likely find that you have regularly occurring needs in most or all of these categories; you can also build your needs cupcake to remind yourself of the ones you experience most often so you don't have to search the whole list when you feel dysregulated.

NEEDS AND STRATEGIES FROM THE ADULT'S PERSPECTIVE

We've already looked at needs from your child's perspective—now let's look at them from yours. When I first start working with parents, they often confuse *needs* and *strategies to meet needs*. This came up during my interview with Sara Dean of *The Shameless Mom Academy* podcast—while working to identify needs, she says (in a number of different ways) that her need is for her seven-year-old to be quieter. Her actual need is for a sense of peace and calm and ease, and one strategy for meeting that need is for her child to be quieter. Sara's child has needs too, which we thought might be about the joy and fun of talking, and potentially a need for connection with other people, since he's an extrovert. Other strategies to meet both of their needs might include Sara asking her child to go outside when he wants to speak loudly, using earplugs or leaving the room to reregulate herself when she's having a hard time, and making sure her child has enough socialization opportunities. By working at the level of needs, we open up a host of potential options to meet those needs that don't seem apparent when we are attached to just one strategy.

Here's another example: I talked with Meg Brunson of the *FamilyPreneur* podcast about her teenager's unwillingness to do basic chores. All Meg asks the teen to do is to wash the dishes after lunch, and it's an uphill struggle every day, so Meg is feeling pretty frustrated. But Meg's real need is not to have the dishes done (which is the strategy she's using to meet her need right now); it's to feel as though she isn't the only person in the family doing all the work. We don't know what the teen's need is yet, but we can hypothesize that she's feeling bored doing the dishes, and also disconnected from her parent. The teen may have a need for autonomy—to make decisions about how to contribute to the family. Meg is also challenged because the teen won't engage in real conversations anymore—most likely because she's learned that sharing her feelings doesn't result in her need being met, so why engage? Meg can meet her needs for collaboration and teamwork and her teen's need for autonomy by asking the child how she would like to contribute to the family's well-being in a way that meets the teen's needs. She may be very willing to do laundry—or even the dishes!—if she feels heard, understood, and respected, and if not doing the chore is genuinely an option.

If you keep track of your feelings and needs for a few days or weeks, your journaling will likely turn up patterns in your physical reactions to your child's behavior, as well as in the needs you're trying to meet. This is incredibly important information, because it means that you snapping at your child doesn't just come out of nowhere, as it may have seemed up to this point. It's not random, and it isn't driven by your child's behavior. Parent Iris says: "My emotions and physical sensations become signposts to my needs." When you can use your physical sensations to identify your needs, you can make a plan for what you'll do when they come up. This might look like:

- My child often asks me to carry them up the stairs, which I was happy to do, but now that I'm pregnant, it makes my back hurt. When they make this request, I feel tightness in my shoulders; that tells me something isn't right. I'm steeling myself for the conflict I know is going to follow, and I feel anxious. I have needs for harmony and ease.

- My child wants me to play with them before I've finished eating dinner. I notice pain in my head, like a headache, and tiredness behind my eyes. I have needs for food, ease, and connection with my partner.

- My child asks me to read *one more book* at bedtime. I sense a tightness in my stomach, and I feel impatient and resistant, and also guilty that I don't want to read. I have needs for self-care and learning from the book I've been reading after my child goes to bed.

When you know your needs, you can plan the strategies you will use in advance so you don't have to make decisions on the fly each time. This reduces what brain scientists call "cognitive load," which basically means you're not spending as much of your energy thinking about how you're going to deal with a situation.

Starter scripts

Here are some phrases to use to try to identify and articulate another person's needs, as well as your own:

> "What were you trying to do when . . . ?"
> "Can you share why . . . wasn't working for you?"
> "Can you tell me why you don't want to . . . ?"
> "I'm trying to . . ."
> "I have a need for . . ."

Ideally, at this point, you're going to have a conversation with your child where you identify their needs and yours, and you will try to find a way to meet both. I'd estimate that 90 percent of the time we disagree with people about whether and how things should be done, we can find ways to meet both of our needs. (More details on how to do this are coming in the next chapter.)

And on the relatively rare occasions when we can't, we can set a boundary.

WE NEED FEWER LIMITS . . . AND A LOT MORE BOUNDARIES

On the occasions when it isn't possible to meet both people's needs in a difficult situation, most of us set *limits* on our child's behavior as a first tool when actually we should use *boundaries*.

We often talk as if limits and boundaries are interchangeable, but they are quite different. We tend to set a lot of limits, because we assume that we're in the right and if the other person would change their behavior, then things would be better. But setting limits on other people's behavior tends to create more trouble for us, because nobody likes it when other people try to change them. The fewer limits we can set on other people's behavior (especially our children's), the easier our lives will be.

Once again, that does *not* mean that we're letting the child run the show. Instead of setting limits, we're going to understand our needs and set boundaries so those needs get met.

For example, you might be thinking to yourself: *I have a rule that everyone has to stay at the table until we're all finished! What's wrong with that?* I would ask you to consider what your real needs are here. Is it for a sense of community over a shared meal? My daughter often likes to sit on the heater near the dinner table with her plate on the floor. She still participates in mealtime conversation, so my need for community is met, and her needs for comfort and autonomy are also met. Win-win, with no limit needed.

LIMITS VERSUS BOUNDARIES

An example of a limit:
"You must stay at the dinner table until everyone has finished eating."

Here, we're trying to change someone else's behavior. Nobody likes it when someone else tries to change their behavior, which is why your child may often protest your limits.

An example of a boundary:
"I'm not willing to get up and play with you until I've finished eating dinner."

We're saying what we aren't willing to do, and the other person is free to respond in whatever way feels appropriate for them. Big feelings may result when you start setting boundaries, but if the boundary is grounded in your needs, you will communicate this both verbally and nonverbally to your child, which will convey that you mean it. They will probably push back much less as a result.

It's also important that we're never looking to a child as the only person who can meet our needs as an adult. We have many avenues of support available to us, perhaps including a partner, friends, parents, mentors, and therapy. We're looking for ways that we can each get our needs met within the context of age-appropriate requests of our child, rather than for our child to be a major source of support for us.

You can refer to the flowchart to the right to help you see when to use each of these tools.

WHEN TO USE THE PROBLEM-SOLVING APPROACH

(And when other tools are more appropriate)

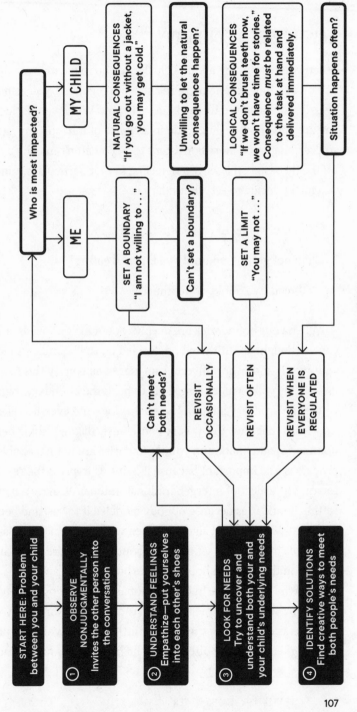

Parenting Beyond Power, by Jen Lumanlan © 2023

HOW TO SET A BOUNDARY

When you're thinking about a challenge you're having with another person at a time when you're relaxed and regulated, you remove the pressure of having to fix the issue *right now*. When you decide what you are and aren't willing to do in advance of it happening again, you're going to be more consistent too—you aren't making a decision on the fly based on how you're feeling in that particular moment. So you might decide to set a boundary like:

> "I'm not willing to carry you up the stairs."
>
> "I'm not getting up until I've finished eating."
>
> "I'll read two books at bedtime."

When your boundaries are deeply rooted in your needs, and you've thought about them and decided on the boundary in advance, your words and your nonverbal language will convey this to your child. They will be much less likely to push the boundary than if you set an arbitrary limit on their behavior—and even less likely as they learn that you're now very consciously distinguishing between boundaries and limits, and your boundaries are not negotiable. This process is also important because it helps us to press the reset button on one aspect of intergenerational trauma. We have a hard time setting boundaries because nobody modeled it for us, and because our needs were walked all over. When we let our children disregard our needs by failing to set our own boundaries, we're perpetuating the lesson that people shouldn't have boundaries—and that's a major reason why we struggle in interpersonal relationships ourselves.

Parent Winnie told me that even though she didn't really want to, she was expected to care for her little brother while her parents worked—now she often jokes she helped raise him because she was the one who picked him up from school and walked him home, made sure he did his homework and checked it, spent her allowance on treats for him, and entertained him on the days school was closed. Winnie's parents expected her to model generosity and graciousness toward her brother and her friends, so she became a people pleaser and did whatever they wanted because it made them happy. Eventually she stopped thinking of herself as an individual with her own needs and desires, and she still struggles with the difference between doing something nice for someone because she cares, and doing it because she feels personally responsible for their emotional state.

Winnie always knew her parents loved her, but in her college years, they started criticizing her for every little thing she did that they didn't agree with. She's now married to someone who was neglected as a child and reports that while they have similar parenting goals, her partner often interacts with their children in a way that doesn't align with those joint values. She has replicated her relationship with her parents in her marriage with a husband who defends himself by pointing out ways *she* has screwed up. Fearful of having an honest conversation about it that might trigger a hurtful attack on her, she has given up on trying to speak out about how the situation is impacting her and is biding her time until the children are old enough to not be harmed by the end of the marriage. Her boundaries are routinely ignored, and while she's providing stability for her children by staying in the marriage, they are also learning by their parent's modeling that setting boundaries is not OK.

By speaking up about our boundaries, we support our children in learning that boundaries are not just OK but are welcome in all kinds of relationships. We want them to be well practiced at understanding and using boundaries by the first time a peer says, "If you want to be my friend, you'll steal the candy," or the first time a romantic partner says, "If you love me, you'll [perform a sex act]." When we teach our children about boundaries, we are helping them to understand needs and that we all should take action based on our needs and values.

Of course, we must also respect our child's boundaries whenever we can. These might include:

- Making sure a child knows they don't have to accept hugs and kisses, even from Grandma, whom they haven't seen in a year—and even from us. They can give respectful greetings in other ways (e.g., high fives).

- Validating their feelings, rather than dismissing or ridiculing them ("But you love your sibling! I know you don't really wish they would go away forever").

- Allowing them to feel "difficult" emotions for as long as they need, without urging them to feel better and demonstrate socially acceptable emotions.

- Not taking food off their plate without asking them first.

- Paying attention to them when they want to talk with us.

This is how we communicate to them: "We are *both* important in this relationship."

OTHER PEOPLE'S REACTIONS TO YOUR BOUNDARIES

It's not spectacularly surprising that we find it difficult to set boundaries. In her book *Set Boundaries, Find Peace*, therapist Nedra Glover Tawwab outlines nine reasons why we find it hard to set boundaries, including that we fear being mean or rude, we feel powerless in the relationship, we believe we can't have boundaries in certain types of relationships, and we get our value from helping others. While Tawwab's book isn't expressly written for women, all of the thought patterns she describes as being reasons why we can't set boundaries are grounded in relationships, which women are taught are their responsibility to maintain. (One of the few male case studies in the book covers boundary issues with money.) If we're rude or mean or exert power, we aren't a Good Girl.

Parent Kelly, who struggled with burnout, has now had lots of practice at setting boundaries with her daughter. She found that when she said, "I can't do this now," her daughter would push back, but when Kelly said, "I won't do that now; I can do . . . ," then her daughter was more likely to accept the proposal. Kelly now knows she isn't responsible for her daughter feeling happy 100 percent of the time, but she is responsible for building a warm and lasting connection, which they create through playing chasing games, going to bed early to read extra stories, and doing housework together. This has dramatically improved Kelly's relationship with her daughter: most of the time, Kelly is able to find solutions that meet both of their needs, but when she can't, she's no longer afraid of her daughter's negative reaction to a boundary—and her daughter pushes back less often as well.

STALEMATES AND BIG FEELINGS

Sometimes no matter how hard you try and how many solutions you bring to problem-solving, your child won't accept any of them and you can't find a strategy that meets everyone's needs. That's when boundaries become most useful, because it allows you to say what you are and aren't willing to do. We can then mourn our inability to find a solution that works for both of us.

I had this conversation recently with my own daughter, who wanted me to read an extra chapter of the book we've been reading at bedtime. I'd been on six hours of calls that day and didn't want to speak anymore. We tried problem-solving, but she concluded: "I just can't think of a way that meets both of our needs!" I told her I thought that if I read her another chapter, I would feel resentful, and I didn't want that. I told her I also wanted her to know what boundaries are and how to set them so she can set them with me and with other people. I acknowledged that it can feel crummy to be on the receiving end of someone else's boundaries, but that's the receiver's issue to navigate.

As long as your boundaries are grounded in your true feelings and needs, there's very little danger you'll set arbitrary boundaries that you'll end up regretting. (It's much more likely that you'll set arbitrary *limits*, which is why we use these as a last-resort tool.) Your child may cry after you set a boundary—which is OK. We aren't trying to completely stop your child from feeling upset; we're trying to move toward living in alignment with your values.

EXERCISE

- What needs do you have right now that aren't being met? Take a look at the List of Needs on page 208 if you need a reference point to get you started. If this is the first time you're thinking about unmet needs, chances are you have quite a lot. Pick one and make a list of five to ten ways that you could meet that need. Is there a way you could meet your need and also meet a need that your child or partner has? If not, can you set a boundary? What would this look like?

- When do you notice feelings of irritation and resentment toward your child? What were they asking you to do when you experienced these feelings? What needs were you trying to meet each time? Write this down in a journal. Look for patterns. You might consider doing this on a daily basis for a week or so.

- What kinds of boundaries do you set with people in your life? Do you think you set enough of them? How does your body feel when you even think about setting a boundary? Can you think of a small boundary that you need to set, and set it, then see what happens?

CHAPTER 6

PROBLEM-SOLVING CONVERSATIONS

A Way to Meet Everyone's Needs

In this chapter, we're going to start stitching all of our new tools together to have Problem-Solving Conversations with our child where we address the challenges between us, not by convincing them of our superior logic or steamrolling them into doing something they don't want to do but by working together to meet both of our needs using new, creative solutions that might never have occurred to you in the past. (And some of these are going to come from your child!)

To review: We understand that people have needs. You have needs and your child has needs. When your needs aren't met, you feel physical sensations that indicate you're becoming frustrated, irritated, or angry, which often build until you snap. When your young child's needs aren't met, they protest, stall, and have what we call "tantrums" because they don't yet have the brain development to out-reason you to get their needs met.

We've learned that sometimes, in the few instances when you can't meet both people's needs, it's appropriate to set a boundary. When we set a boundary, we're not trying to change someone else's behavior (that would be a limit); we're just saying what we are and aren't willing to do. When we set a boundary, what we're essentially saying to our child is: "I see you have a need, and I also have a need, and right now, I don't see a way to meet both of those needs so, in this instance, I'm going to make sure my need gets met." There are plenty of times when boundaries are an appropriate tool to use.

But the really exciting part about the Problem-Solving Approach is that it opens up the possibility that both people having a conflict in a relationship can get their needs met.

I know this is a really hard thing to get our heads around. Eurocentric, and particularly American, culture teaches us that when there's a conflict, someone wins and someone loses. It's very uncommon for US-originated sporting contests to result in a tie— perhaps that's why soccer has never really caught on here? Our legal system creates a winner and a loser rather than healing and reconciliation. When two people disagree, the person who has the superior logic (or better gaslighting skills) "wins," and their version of what happened and what to do next are accepted. It's really difficult to imagine that we might actually come out of a conflict in a way that meets both people's needs.

When we don't understand the other person's needs—or even our own needs!—trying to find solutions to problems that work for both people is virtually impossible. We find ourselves negotiating over competing strategies, like: "I want to go to the park" and "I want to stay home." It seems like there's nowhere to go from here that works for everyone.

MANY WAYS TO MEET NEEDS

The awesome thing about needs is that there are hundreds of ways to meet each of them. Here's the start of a list of ideas for strategies that meet a need for connection:

- A hug
- A kiss
- A back rub
- Call a loved one
- Go for a walk with a friend
- Do something special for another person
- Express appreciation for something another person has done
- Look them in the eye when you're talking with them
- Remember a previous connecting conversation with them
- Learn how they like to receive love and meet that need
- Share something interesting that happened to you
- Be honest about how you're feeling
- Don't interrupt them
- Do something new together
- Play a game
- Be silly together
- Show them you're on their side
- Tell them you love them
- Meet someone new

I could go on and on; you can probably immediately identify some ideas that I've missed. If we get hung up on a particular strategy ("I have to go for a walk with a friend") and our child wants to ride their bike at the park, it can seem like there's no way to meet both needs. Conflict results when the parent either asserts their desire (and the child resists) or they roll over and deliver on the child's desire (and resent it). We go through most of our days with our needs repeatedly not being met, and then we flip our lid with our kid when we can't take it anymore.

So let's work this one through. I want to take a walk with my friend: that's a strategy. What's the underlying need I'm trying to meet? Mainly connection, but perhaps I also have a need for exercise and I was planning to do both at once. My child wants to ride their bike: that's a strategy. Their underlying needs might be for movement, joy, and excitement. So how can we meet both people's needs? Here are some ideas:

- My friend and I walk together while my child rides in front of us.

- We all go for a bike ride together and bring a picnic; my friend and I chat while we snack and my child plays on the playground.

- We all go for a walk together.

- I meet my friend for a walk, and my child goes to a park with my partner.

- I chat with my friend on the phone and then go for a run while my child rides alongside.

Do you see how working at the level of needs opens up options where it seemed like none had existed before? It's almost like magic!

MAKING REQUESTS TO GET OUR NEEDS MET

When we've identified each person's needs, the next thing to do is to make a request. There are three key features of a request:

1. It's stated in clear terms, and it asks the other person to do something rather than *not* do something.

2. It's specific enough to be doable in the near future.

3. It is not a demand. The other person can say no without fear of retribution.

Let's look at each of these in turn.

When we make a request in clear terms, we aren't saying things like: "I wish you would pick up after yourself." Here, the "I wish" helps the asker to avoid actually making a request at all. And what does "pick up after yourself" mean? Put your shoes in the closet? Put your clothes in the hamper? Put your toys away? It's not clear. We're also not saying what we *don't* want: "Don't leave your shoes out," "Don't leave your clothes on the floor," or "Don't leave your toys where people can trip over them."

When we ask for the specific thing we want, then the other person can decide whether or not they're willing to do it. This might look like: "Would you be willing to put your shoes in the closet?" or "Would you be willing to play that game outside?" As you get more used to having Problem-Solving Conversations with your child, you may not even need to make formal requests. One of you might just come up with an idea, and the other realizes immediately it will meet their needs, and you just agree to do it.

The third element of a request is feeling free to say no without fear of retribution. This means that you really are *asking* them, not telling them! This isn't something we're often accustomed to doing with our children. We might have learned that we should offer a child two choices that are both acceptable to us, which isn't really the same: in that scenario, we haven't taken the time to understand the child's needs, so we don't know if *any* of the ideas we're proposing meet their needs. This is why parents find this approach often "doesn't work"—because the child is still resisting doing something that doesn't meet their needs.

If the child declines our request, we can't punish them ("Are you willing to . . . ? No? Then go to your room!"); we can't give ultimatums ("Are you willing to . . . ? No? Well, then you have to . . ."); and we can't guilt-trip them into it ("Are you willing to. . . . ? No? Well, now Mama's going to be really sad . . ."). This is where we're really moving into "power with" rather than "power over" territory. It can be scary as a parent to move away from telling our child to do things and asking them instead.

We're so afraid of that "no"! We've been trained to associate "no" with rejection—rejection of our idea as well as rejection of us as people. But when we hear a "no" in this context, it isn't a rejection of us; it's just a way of expressing: "That suggestion didn't meet my need." Instead of thinking of a "no" as a door closing, think of it as another door opening: it's an opportunity to try again. There is probably another solution that meets everyone's needs, and in working with us to find it, our child practices being in relationship with others where everyone's needs are truly respected and met. This is how the Problem-Solving Approach helps us today and gives our children the opportunity to practice being in right relationship with all people, even those who have very different needs from us.

Starter scripts

Here are some ways to open up a request:

> "Would you be willing to . . . ?"
>
> "If I were to . . . , would that help?"
>
> "Do you think we could try . . . ?"

WHY WE STRUGGLE WITH MAKING REQUESTS

Parents often struggle with making requests, for a few reasons. Firstly, there are circumstances where a boundary or a limit is more appropriate. Maybe you've already gotten up three times during dinner, and you are *not* willing to get up a fourth time. You might offer that the child can get the blue cup if they want to, but *you* are not going to do it (a boundary). Or your young child is exploring the house and discovers an electrical outlet for the first time, and you tell them not to touch it (a limit). Perhaps you remove them from the area and plan to invest in some outlet covers so the environment provides the limit instead of you the next time.

If you're new to this approach, then it's likely there are a whole lot of situations where, right now, limits seem like your only options. In a Setting Loving (& Effective!) Limits workshop that I run, I first ask participants to keep track of how many limits they set in a day— and they are universally shocked by the result. They find they've been setting limits tens and sometimes hundreds of times a day and that these limits have no connection to their values as parents and as a family. Perhaps there are some situations where you can immediately see your need and your child's need, and you jump in and make a request: "Would you be willing to run around outside instead of in the house?" But perhaps there are others where you see the needs . . . and yet you just can't bring yourself to use this method. You're worried that your partner isn't on board, that your in-laws will judge you, that your child will do something that isn't "good for them." And that's OK! You don't have to do it all at once. Just start by using the tools that do feel comfortable right now, and go from there.

PROBLEM-SOLVING CONVERSATIONS IN ACTION

For your first attempt at a Problem-Solving Conversation, I always recommend choosing a topic that isn't the one that's currently the biggest struggle you're having with your child, and discussing it a time when you *haven't* just had a disagreement about it. If you're both really riled up about something, it's going to be more difficult to practice this new method at the same time as you're navigating both of your amped-up feelings. Wait until everyone is calm and fed and rested while these tools are still new to you. As you become more comfortable with the Problem-Solving Approach, you can use it at the beginning of a situation that is turning into a conflict to find a path forward that works for both of you in the moment.

The diagram on the facing page will help you envision how a Problem-Solving Conversation works.

HOW TO SOLVE PROBLEMS BETWEEN YOU AND YOUR CHILD

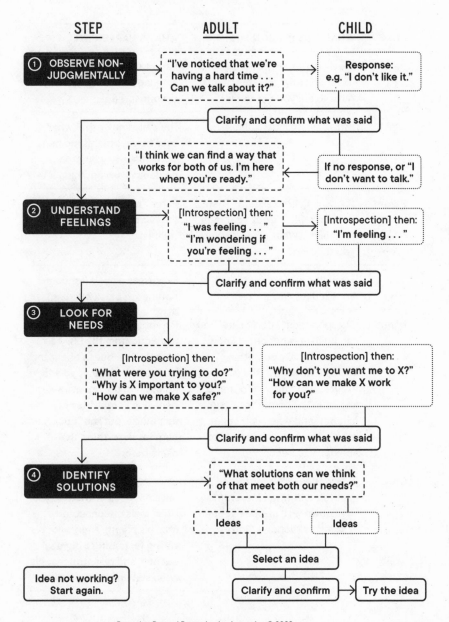

STEP   **ADULT**   **CHILD**

① OBSERVE NON-JUDGMENTALLY

"I've noticed that we're having a hard time . . . Can we talk about it?"

Response: e.g. "I don't like it."

Clarify and confirm what was said

"I think we can find a way that works for both of us. I'm here when you're ready."

If no response, or "I don't want to talk."

② UNDERSTAND FEELINGS

[Introspection] then: "I was feeling . . ." "I'm wondering if you're feeling . . ."

[Introspection] then: "I'm feeling . . ."

Clarify and confirm what was said

③ LOOK FOR NEEDS

[Introspection] then: "What were you trying to do?" "Why is X important to you?" "How can we make X safe?"

[Introspection] then: "Why don't you want me to X?" "How can we make X work for you?"

Clarify and confirm what was said

④ IDENTIFY SOLUTIONS

"What solutions can we think of that meet both our needs?"

Ideas

Ideas

Select an idea

Idea not working? Start again.

Clarify and confirm → Try the idea

Here's an example of how this conversation might have gone in the past, when a preschooler has just hit their toddler sibling:

ROLE	WHAT THIS PERSON MIGHT SAY	WHAT'S HAPPENING
Parent	"Hey! Don't smack your sister like that! How many times do I have to tell you not to hit?"	Parent uses judgmental language. Parent is already dysregulated.
Child	[Stays silent; looks sullen]	The child knows that whatever he says in this moment won't make any difference, so he doesn't say anything.
Parent	[Consoling little sister:] "There, there; it's OK. It's not your fault." [To child:] "What on earth were you thinking?"	Parent takes sides with the "victim" rather than the "aggressor."
Child	[Avoiding eye contact:] "She knocked my tower over."	Expresses a need (for competence in block building).
Parent	[Exasperated:] "I don't care! You can build another one! I know it's hard to have something knocked down, but that's no excuse: *Don't hit your sister!* Go and sit in the corner for three minutes, and when you come back, you'd better be ready to apologize to her."	Parent is not able to see the world from the child's perspective, doesn't hear the expression of the need and focuses on the undesirable behavior. Parent tries to empathize, but the "but" negates everything that came before it.
Child	[Sits in the corner for three minutes, and when he returns, eyes downcast, mutters vaguely in sister's direction:] "Sorry."	Child's feelings and needs have not been acknowledged. Child feels disconnected from his parent, angry with his sibling for making a big deal out of it, and resentful that his need still isn't being met.

In this interaction the parent jumped in and instantly judged the dispute, pronouncing one child the "victim" and the other the "aggressor." The child has learned that a rhetorical question ("How many times do I have to tell you not to hit?") isn't actually an invitation to share; it's an admonition and is intended to shame them into changing their behavior. They know they have to respond when their parent asks "What on earth were you thinking?" because their parent will keep asking until they get an answer, but this is not a safe space. The child isn't going to reveal anything about their true feelings or needs. By making the child go into time-out, the parent withdraws their affection and connection from the child until their behavior complies with the parent's wishes. The child does this with a forced apology, and the situation seems superficially "fixed," except that the parent is still frustrated, and the child is now feeling both angry and resentful toward their sibling—and probably toward their parent too.

In Chapter 8, we'll look at what to do when you're actually in the difficult moments. For now, let's focus on how to use the tools we've been learning so we can have a different kind of conversation some time *after* the difficult interaction has happened, which is when it's easiest to practice your new skills:

ROLE	WHAT THIS PERSON MIGHT SAY	WHAT'S HAPPENING
Parent	"Hey, I noticed we've been having a hard time when your toys are out in the living room. Would it be OK if we chat about it?"	Parent observes using non-judgmental language; invites the child to participate in a discussion; and is willing to not have the discussion if the child declines.
Child	"OK."	Child expresses their willingness to participate in the conversation.

ROLE	WHAT THIS PERSON MIGHT SAY	WHAT'S HAPPENING
Parent	"It seems like sometimes we have trouble when your toys are on the floor and your little sister is in the room. She's always really interested in what you're doing, right? And sometimes she knocks your tower over when you're building. What's going on for you when that happens?"	Parent continues the non-judgmental observation of the situation and invites the child to share their feelings without directly asking.
Child	"I don't like it when she knocks my stuff over!"	Child expresses an idea that we can use to extrapolate their feelings: perhaps tense and anxious as little sister approaches, and frustrated and angry as she knocks his tower down.
Parent	"Oh, I hear you! I bet it's really tough to have to keep an eye out for her all the time, and it must be frustrating to have to start all over again when she knocks your stuff over or takes it."	Parent shows they can understand the world from the child's perspective and validates his feelings.
Child	"Yeah!"	Child indicates that parent has correctly identified his feelings.

ROLE	WHAT THIS PERSON MIGHT SAY	WHAT'S HAPPENING
Parent	"Yeah, I would have a hard time with that too. And I know I feel overwhelmed when you feel angry with her and hit her because I need to keep her safe. What were you trying to do yesterday when she came in?"	Parent identifies their feeling (overwhelmed) and need (safety for the younger child; there may also be other needs, perhaps related to their childhood experiences, that are important for the parent to acknowledge, but we don't necessarily want to tell the child). Parent asks about the child's need.
Child	"I was trying to build the tallest tower ever!"	Parent extrapolates that the child has needs for competence (building a tall tower), space, and freedom (from interference by the younger sibling).
Parent	"Oh, that sounds like so much fun! What do you think your sister was trying to do when she came in?"	Parent empathizes and scaffolds the child's ability to understand another person's needs.
Child	"I think she wanted to help, but she's so annoying! She always takes my stuff!"	Child has identified one of his sibling's needs: for contribution.
Parent	"If I were you, I would probably find that annoying too. I think she does want to help. I wonder if she also just wanted to be close to you? She really loves you."	Parent shows they understand the child's needs and identifies another of the sibling's needs: for connection.
Child	"I know. But I still don't want her to do it."	Child empathizes with his sibling and restates his need.

ROLE	WHAT THIS PERSON MIGHT SAY	WHAT'S HAPPENING
Parent	"I hear you. It sounds like you wanted to build a really tall tower, and you wanted space to do that. And you also wanted the freedom to do it without your sister messing things up. Is that right?"	Parent states what they believe the child's needs to be, and asks for confirmation.
Child	"Yeah."	Child confirms that parent has identified his needs.
Parent	"OK. And I need to know that your sister is safe, and she wants to help and spend time with you. I wonder what we could do that can meet everyone's needs?"	Parent identifies the other two people's needs and offers the possibility of meeting everyone's needs.
Child	"I don't know."	Child is new to this method and doesn't know what to suggest.
Parent	"Well, one option I see would be that you could build important stuff in your room with the door closed. Then your sister wouldn't be able to mess up your tower."	Parent is new to this method and suggests an idea that doesn't actually meet everyone's needs—it meets the parent's and this child's needs, but not the sibling's needs for connection and contribution.
Child	"Yeah, but I don't want to be by myself in my room all the time."	Child surfaces another need: for community with the family by being in proximity to them.

ROLE	WHAT THIS PERSON MIGHT SAY	WHAT'S HAPPENING
Parent	"Mmm, you're right. What if we put up the old baby gates around an area in the living room, and you could build in there? You could always pass stuff through to your sister when she wants to help, but she wouldn't be able to get to your towers. And you'd still be in the living room where we all hang out. Could that work for you?"	Parent identifies an idea that seems to meet everyone's needs.
Child	"Yeah! And I could put a few blocks out for her to play with so she could 'help' with those."	Child adds their own idea to meet his sibling's need.
Parent	"I think she'd love that. Will you come and help me get the baby gates out?"	Parent moves toward the solution that works for everyone.
Child	"Sure!"	Child willingly collaborates.

A few important things happened in this conversation. Firstly, · the parent avoided using the word "but." I'm sure you've heard this when people say something like: "I know this is important to you, but . . ." That "but" is a key word: it says that whatever is coming after is really what matters; whatever connecting statement came before is much less important. That "but" leaves us feeling unheard and disconnected from the person we're talking with, in the precise moment when we need connection so badly—our feelings are invalidated, and this can itself cause a child (and even an adult!) to melt down.

Secondly, many children clam up when we start asking them about their feelings, and if we just come out and ask them about their needs, then they likely won't know what to say. The parents I work with have found that questions like "What was going on for you when that happened?" is an effective way to uncover feelings, while "What were you trying to do?" can get us to an understanding of their needs in a way that most children are usually able to answer.

Finally, the parent tried to put all the needs on the table. This is really critical. We don't necessarily have to tell our children all of *our* needs, especially if these are rooted in trauma that we've experienced in childhood or adulthood. Perhaps our own parent used to sit idly by while our older sibling beat the crap out of us, and we're terrified that we're going to let the same dynamic happen in our home, so we squash anything that looks like anger. We're not necessarily going to tell our child that, but we need to acknowledge all the things that are causing us to react to our child's difficult behavior and get support from other adults if necessary.

When we don't understand all of the needs at play, the potential solutions we generate and the requests we make won't "stick":

- If *your child's need* isn't met, then they might agree to the request in the moment because they feel guilt or shame or fear of punishment or rejection, but when the situation comes up again, they won't hold up their end of the bargain (and they're less likely to want to engage in a Problem-Solving Conversation with you next time).
- If *your need* isn't met, then when you put the solution into practice, you're most likely going to feel annoyance and resentment (and you'll think: *This problem-solving stuff doesn't work!*).

If we can accurately identify each person's needs, we're likely to be able to find a solution that works for both of us—if we can think creatively enough about the situation and open ourselves up to the possibility that an idea we might not have previously considered could actually meet our needs.

In the previous example, the parent offered most of the potential solutions, and you might have to do this as well when you and your child are new to this work. But over time, they'll get used to working with you in this way, and they will start producing surprisingly creative ideas that also meet your needs.

Here's an example of how it might work:

ROLE	WHAT THIS PERSON MIGHT SAY	WHAT'S HAPPENING
Parent	"I see you jumping from one part of the deck to the other. The steps are right in front of you, and I'm worried that you might jump too far and fall down them."	Parent observes the situation nonjudgmentally and states their feeling (worry) about what could happen and their need (for their child's safety).
Child	"I'm jumping between the light-colored planks so I can mark how far I've jumped!"	Child expresses their needs: for competence in jumping, as well as movement and joy.
Parent	"Hmm . . . so what could we do that meets both of our needs?"	Parent opens up the possibility that both people's needs can be met.
Child	"I could mark where I'm jumping with stones instead of planks, and then I could jump over there."	Child proposes an alternate solution.

ROLE	WHAT THIS PERSON MIGHT SAY	WHAT'S HAPPENING
Parent	"If you mark where you're jumping, I'm concerned that you might jump right onto the stones and slip and hurt yourself. What if you put the stones off to the side of where you're jumping instead?"	Parent expresses that the first solution proposed doesn't meet their need and suggests a modification of the solution.
Child	"OK!"	Child accepts the solution; both people's needs are met.

The key here is that the parent accurately identified their own need. If the parent's need was for quiet so they could read or work, changing the nearby location and using stones wouldn't "work" because the parent's need wouldn't be met. In this case, solutions like the child jumping farther down the garden or the parent reading or working indoors could become options. Very often, we only consider ways that our children could change their behavior to meet our needs, but offering to change our own behavior both helps the child to feel more invested in the process and makes more potential options available.

This is the basic process for Problem-Solving Conversations. On the facing page is a template you can use to approach any problem you're having with your child that's based on the flowchart on page 123. Download a full-sheet template to address each challenge you're having at https://www.YourParentingMojo.com/BookBonuses.

PROBLEM-SOLVING TEMPLATE

Use the starter scripts on page 209 to help if you need to.

Step 1: Make a nonjudgmental observation of the situation

State the issue as a video camera would see it, and request the child's permission to discuss it. Don't use: "You always . . ." or "You never . . ." or use hot-button words like "mess," "late," or "refuse."

Step 2: Understand each person's feelings

Don't use "I feel like," which leads to judgments rather than feelings. Refer to the List of Feelings starting on page 206 if you need a reminder.

My feelings:

My child's feelings:

Step 3: Understand each person's needs

Don't mix up needs and strategies to meet those needs. "I want to be alone" is one strategy for self-care. Use the List of Needs on page 208 if you need help.

My needs:

My child's needs:

Step 4: Identify potential solutions that could meet both people's needs

Write down as many ideas as you and your child can think of. Then review the ideas to see which solutions could really meet both of your needs.

WHAT TO DO WHEN THE SHIT IS
REALLY HITTING THE FAN

I do want to reiterate that Problem-Solving Conversations are best done out of the heat of the moment when everyone is calm and regulated. It's virtually impossible for you or your child to practice a new skill when you're both riled up from a recent disagreement; stopping hitting and kicking with words is rarely effective. When this happens, your best strategies are to:

Regulate yourself

If your own physical signals are indicating that you're becoming dysregulated, do what you can to regulate yourself first. There are some suggestions in Chapter 7 to help you out.

Keep everyone safe

If you're sitting down and you're being hit, stand up. If you can block the hit, do that and say: "I won't let you hit" (don't say this if the child has already hit you; if they have, say: "I don't want to be hit").

If children are hitting each other, try to remove one of them from the situation or otherwise separate them.

Get out of the situation as gracefully as you can

If possible, try to be present with your child to the extent that they want you to be present while their big feelings are ongoing and while keeping your body safe. Earplugs or noise-canceling headphones can be really helpful in making this feel more doable if you are sensitive to loud noises and your child makes a lot of them.

If you need space, try to get it by standing up and creating a sense of space for yourself if possible, rather than withdrawing to another room. Separation can cause many children to feel more dysregulated, which keeps the cycle going.

If you can, try to empathize with the feelings your child is expressing. If you can't, try to just stay present and acknowledge: "We're having a hard time right now." It *will* pass.

Make a plan to reconnect later

It can be helpful to use a natural separation point to set a plan for later reconnection. When my daughter was in day care, after difficult mornings, I would say: "We had a tough morning, huh? Let's talk about it later, OK?" This *must* be delivered in a calm, compassionate, collaborative tone. It isn't a threat; it's a promise to come back together later to reconnect and see if we can find a path forward that meets both of our needs. You can do the same at bedtime after a difficult evening to plan for a next-day reconnection.

PROBLEM-SOLVING WITH MORE THAN ONE PERSON

Parents who are new to this method sometimes wonder how they can use this approach with more than one person. Parent Denise's daughter wanted to make a "potion" (needs for joy, play, and creativity), while Denise was feeling cautious because they were going to leave the house soon and she needed ease and collaboration in that transition. Her husband was feeling tired, and had needs for ease and order in their small apartment without him having to clean up after their child. Because her family has been using the Problem-Solving Approach for four years now, they no longer needed to go through the process of identifying each person's feelings and needs out loud; they understood them implicitly because they have what Denise describes as a "foundation of respect and trust." In just a few minutes, they found a solution that worked for everyone: making the potion in the bathroom with a towel on the floor and setting a timer for ten minutes.

One of the best rewards of practicing this approach with children is when they start to use it between themselves. I interviewed parents Adrianna and Tim on my podcast, who described how Adrianna first started by identifying five-year-old Bodhi's needs and working to meet these. Soon afterward, when Tim was having a hard time putting Bodhi to bed, Bodhi said: "Wait; Mom would ask me what my needs were and how we can meet both of our needs!" It turned out that Bodhi was worried he would forget what colors he wanted to use in his drawing the next day, so Tim made a list for him, and then Bodhi went right to bed.

Up to that point, Adrianna was about at her wit's end with her two children fighting. She couldn't even step away to pee without them screaming at and hitting each other. Not long after the bedtime success, three-year-old Remi came into the room where Bodhi was drawing and started coloring on Bodhi's paper. Bodhi said: "Are you feeling sad because we didn't get to play together today? How about we play for five minutes, and then I'll come back and work on my drawing?" They played together for five minutes and then worked collaboratively alongside each other. These tools also have improved Adrianna and Tim's relationship, and even the ways that Tim works with his colleagues. They really do make life easier!

The next chapter will help you to overcome some common challenges with problem-solving so you can hit the ground running.

CHAPTER 7:

COMMON DIFFICULTIES WITH PROBLEM-SOLVING CONVERSATIONS

And How to Address Each One

I've helped a lot of parents to implement these strategies, and it's very common for them to run into problems when they start to put them into practice. After all, this is pretty different from the way we were raised, right? There are two main "buckets" of reasons why we have problems—the first is related to the triggered feelings we get when our child asserts their needs, because it reminds us of how our needs were not met as children, so we'll look at that first.

Then, once we start problem-solving, we often stumble in how we implement the strategies with our child—so we'll go through some common challenges parents face in actually using the Problem-Solving Approach and how to address each of these.

CHALLENGES COMING FROM THE PARENT'S EXPERIENCE

As we've learned, many of us were raised in ways that didn't meet our needs. Dr. Miki Kashtan argues that "the basic flaw of childrearing is that it masquerades as being for the child's good, when in reality the practices are largely geared toward the adults' perspective." In other words: what the child really needs is less important than what the parent needs, what the parent thinks is good for the child, the parent's desire for ease and peace of mind now and in the future, and their concern for social acceptability ("Will my in-laws think I'm raising a feral child?").

Our parents disregarded our needs because our culture told them that that's what good parents do. This may have been overt, as when a parent refuses to accept a child's sexuality or gender identity. Or perhaps it was quite subtle: our parent became a little distant when we weren't outgoing enough or friendly enough or masculine/feminine enough. Or maybe it was somewhere in between, which they might have shown by rewarding us with praise, affection, or even money for good grades and complying with their wishes, and punished us with the removal of their time or affection, or withdrawing privileges for not getting on well with siblings or "slacking" in school.

Dr. Bessel van der Kolk, author of *The Body Keeps the Score*, told me that particularly when we're young, we "make meaning" from confusing, traumatizing events by blaming ourselves. We develop self-hatred and think: "this must have happened to me because I was a bad person, and people treat me like a bad person." Even if our parents were doing the best they could, they most likely didn't see or meet all of our needs, because nobody ever taught them how to do it. Instead, when we asserted our needs we were shut down, so we panic when we hear our child assert their needs today—because their behavior causes us to revisit that old trauma of rejection by our parents.

Here are some of the kinds of things children do that the parents I work with find hard to hear, and the reasons why:

CHILD SAYS OR DOES	PARENT FINDS THIS TRIGGERING BECAUSE
"I want an ice cream"	They would have been punished for not saying "please."
Leaves a trail of toys in their wake	Their own parent screamed at them for making a mess.
Makes holiday cards for friends that get smudged	Their mom used to check their homework, and if the page was smudged, or had scribbles or bent corners, she would rip off the page and tell them to start over again.
"I can't walk anymore"	Their own parent told them they were lazy and that they had to walk, when they really were tired.
Asks to play. Says, "Mom, Mom, Mom!"	They weren't allowed to do something as frivolous as playing, or anything that came across as needy or nagging.
Sets a boundary with others in a tone that could be perceived as "rude"	They were taught that having boundaries isn't as important as making others happy and comfortable.

CHILD SAYS OR DOES	PARENT FINDS THIS TRIGGERING BECAUSE
Uses an "inappropriate" tone	They got yelled at when they displayed any tone that sounded like an "attitude."
"I hate you!"	Their own parent spanked or punished them for saying that.
Loudly expresses anger	Whenever they expressed anger as a child, their own parent reacted by putting them in time-out; using intense, mean-spirited sarcasm; putting on an angry face; and/or saying: "Ooh, look at you, the world must be so bad, boo-hoo."

Certainly, childhood trauma isn't the only reason we find our children's behavior difficult to navigate—we can get flooded when we haven't had our current needs met (like sleep, self-care, and exercise)—but among the parents I work with, childhood trauma is a very, very common reason why parents have a hard time shifting their interactions with their children.

If you see this pattern showing up in your own life, it's really important that you get support. Therapy can be very helpful if you're really struggling, and a lot of parents make shifts in a workshop that I run called Taming Your Triggers. It's important to know that unless you specifically make an attempt to shift this pattern, it is likely to repeat into the next generation in the ways you interact with *your* child. There are never any guarantees in parenting, and some people who have experienced trauma do go on to raise fulfilled children with no outside support, but it's not as common as we would hope. What happened to you is not your *fault*, but it is your *responsibility* to do something about it if you want to have different interactions with your own child.

In the meantime, on the following pages, I have compiled some resources and ideas that may help, broken down into work you can do before, during, and after difficult moments.

Work to do in advance: Healing from trauma you've experienced

- The book *How to Stop Losing Your Sh*t with Your Kids* is an excellent, evidence-based resource, and may be enough for some people to move the needle on this topic, although parents often find that they need more than just new *knowledge* to navigate their triggered feelings—they need to make a shift that happens *in their body*, which more often happens through learning in community.

- Check in regularly with what's going on in your body. Notice when you're feeling well and rested and renewed, and when you're feeling depleted and stressed and overwhelmed. How do these feelings show up in your body? When you can notice these sensations as an indicator that things aren't right for you *before you explode*, you can take action to prevent the explosion.

- Engage in self-care. Not the manicure kind, but the truly renewing, often community-based kind (see the Afterword on page 183 for more on this).

- Plan to practice self-compassion: We're human, and we *will* mess up! Instead of getting caught flat-footed, let's plan for what we'll do when we fail. We can acknowledge the reasons we find this difficult ("Given everything I've experienced, it's no wonder I find this hard"). And we can remind ourselves that any reasonable person would struggle and that we can experience the struggle in this moment ("I'm having a hard time") without getting caught up in the stories our brain wants to tell us ("I'm a terrible parent and I'm *never* going to be better at this!").

- Make sure you're asking your child to do things that are developmentally appropriate (review the list starting on page 62 if needed).

- For issues that come up over and over again, make a plan for how you will navigate them next time. Handling them in the heat of the moment puts more stress on all of you. Your plan should be based in your values. Do you have values related to your child's body autonomy? And is your conflict about them wanting to choose what clothes they wear (or whether they wear clothes at all at home)? How does the way you've been approaching this align with your values? What kinds of things would you need to do to bring your interactions with your child more into alignment with your values?

Work to do in the moment: Create, and then use, a pause

- Try to create a pause between your child's behavior and your response. Here are some centering exercises you can use to bring yourself back to the present in a stressful situation. In the beginning, you'll forget to use them. Then you'll remember and still not be able to use them. Eventually you'll remember and create a split second of a pause, and this will lengthen into a breath. In a breath, you can make a different decision. Here are some ways to begin creating a pause:

  - Keep a hair tie on one wrist and transfer it to the other wrist when you're triggered. The hair tie is a visual reminder of your values and intention, and the transfer helps to create the pause.

  - Take a deep breath.

- Put sticky notes up around the house with short statements about your values (e.g., "My relationship with my child is the most important thing") and glance at them when you feel triggered.

- Before you go to bed each night, put your hand on your heart and feel your calm, steady heartbeat. When you feel triggered by your child, put your hand on your heart, which will remind your body of what it's like to feel calm.

- Reach out and touch something around you: the smoothness of the table, or the softness of a stuffed animal (which sounds strange but can be really comforting!).

- Pick a color and look for everything around you that is that color.

- Count something (like all the purple objects in the room).

- Recognize that you *can* make a decision in these moments. In Acceptance and Commitment Therapy, this is called a choice point. Envision yourself at a point with two potential paths ahead of you. One takes you in the direction you've gone down before, away from your values. The other takes you in a new direction, toward your values. You get to choose which path you take.

- If you're very new to problem-solving, don't try to have a conversation when you're triggered or flooded. You can't empathize with someone else, never mind generate new, creative solutions to challenges, when you're already dysregulated.

- You don't have to make an instant decision. It's fine to tell your child: "I'm thinking about it."

- If you're regulated enough, tell them *why* you don't want them to do the activity (this is your need) and try to understand why they want to do it (their need). What ideas can you come up with together to make it safer or more acceptable? Can you make a request?

- If things are heating up, you could say: "We're having a really hard time right now, huh?" and sit down with them to take a break before you make any decisions. If things are getting difficult quickly, refer to the "What to Do When the Shit Is Really Hitting the Fan" section on page 134.

Work to do afterward: Make amends with your child

When we mess up, we often want to sweep it under the rug; if the child seems to have forgotten, we certainly don't want to bring it up again. When we make amends by retelling the story, we give the child the opportunity to integrate the difficult memories so they won't become flooding/triggering to our children in adulthood like our own memories are to us.

These techniques can also help you to get out of the stories you're telling yourself about how your child is so difficult, irritating, or irresponsible and how you're such a terrible parent so you can reconnect with your values and respond instead of just reacting. This might look like:

Parent: "I was in the shower, and you were playing with the glitter . . ."

Child: "And it slipped out of my hand!"

Parent: "And it went all over the floor!"

Child: "I was scared."

Parent: "Why were you scared?"

Child: "I thought you'd be angry."

Parent: "And then I came out of the shower and saw it on the floor, and I was suddenly so angry, I shouted at you!"

Child: [starts crying]

Parent: "I'm so sorry I shouted. I shouldn't have done that. I was frustrated because we were in a rush to get out of the house, but that's no excuse for yelling at you. I'm really sorry. Next time I feel like yelling, I'm going to try to take a deep breath first, OK?"

Child: "OK."

CHALLENGES WITH THE PROBLEM-SOLVING PROCESS

Here are some of the challenges I commonly see parents face when they're new to implementing problem-solving, and how to address each one:

1 **We focus on trying to change the child's behavior.** When we see the behavior as the problem, we're not truly being collaborative with our child: we're not saying "*we* have a problem"; we're saying "*you* have a problem." When we go into one of these conversations with an agenda about someone else needing to do something differently while we keep doing what we've always done, it's very difficult to generate solutions that work for everyone.

Solution: Try to shift your thinking from seeing your child's behavior as being the problem that needs fixing to being something that is expressing your child's feelings and needs in the best, most competent way they know how. When you're talking with your child, don't focus on the behavior you wish were different. Pull them in close (if they'll let you, and it seems like it would feel good to them) and say: "You're having a really hard time right now, huh?" Or if you're both dysregulated, say: "We're having a really hard time right now, huh?" This provides the space to focus on the problem, not the behavior, together.

2   **We judge the child's behavior.** We might say things like "You always . . ." or "You never . . ." It's easy to see the effects of judging when we think about how it feels when it's done to us. Just take a statement you've said to your child that starts with: "You're always . . ." or "You never . . ." or even "You're such a . . ." or "You're so . . ." Then imagine your partner or another adult saying it to you. Does it make you want to cooperate with them?

   Solution: Instead of judging the child, just say what you see. Replace "Your room is so messy!" with "I see toys on the floor!" Replace "You never put your shoes away!" with "I see shoes by the door!" Saying what you see removes judgment, which creates space between the difficult event and your own thoughts about it. Many parents find that they can then have more compassion for their child's experience and can more easily identify the need their child was trying to meet in doing the thing the parent found difficult.

3 **We don't take the time to understand the child's needs.** This issue has probably been irritating us for a while now, and we just want to get to a solution as fast as possible, right? We ask them how they're feeling and empathize, and it seems like the child is willing to work with us (great!), so we start throwing solutions out and our child doesn't like any of them, or we agree to one and then it doesn't "work"—because we never understood the child's true need. Then the child ends up feeling steamrolled into a solution and less likely to want to engage in a Problem-Solving Conversation again in the future. The next time you ask them how they're feeling about something, they might not want to tell you because they know it will only lead to you imposing a solution on them.

   Solution: Take time to understand both your child's needs and your needs before you start generating potential solutions. (Even the process of understanding your own needs may help you to see new solutions.)

4 **We can't understand the child's needs.** When parents are new to this approach, it's pretty common to mistake *solutions* or *strategies* for *needs*. Remember: jumping on the sofa isn't a need; it's a strategy to meet the needs of movement, play, and joy. Getting a child to stop jumping on the sofa isn't a need; it's a strategy to meet the needs of quiet, safety, and protection (of the furniture). When we introduce the idea of needs, our child might say: "I need to jump on the sofa!" and it's our job to understand what the child's real need is. Even with a preverbal child, we can often guess the child's needs for food/drink, joy, play, independence, and autonomy. When a parent says: "I don't know what the need is," this often seems to be code for: "It's

scary to understand the need because I might not be willing to meet it since I've been conditioned to think that it's my job to make my child comply with my wishes."

Solution: Use what you know about the child's behavior and personality, as well as what they're telling you, to make a hypothesis about what their need is. Look to their needs cupcake to see if you think it might be any of the top three to five needs, and then the next three to five; then look at the rest of the cupcake. Don't forget to identify your need—which, again, is *not* "to make the child do what I want" or any other specific strategy. Now, is there a way that both people's needs can be met?

5   **We decide what the "correct" solution is in advance.** Pretty often, we feel that we already know the answer to a problem, and we think that if we can just get our child to see it our way, things will be better. But by focusing on meeting needs, we find we can generate all kinds of solutions that didn't seem relevant or useful before.

Solution: With a very young child, we may be the one who provides suggestions for ways to solve the problem, but as soon as the child is able to suggest their own solution, we should grab hold of it with both hands and make it work if it's even vaguely possible. This will help the child to see that we really do value their input and will use it if we can.

6   **We try to fix the issue when everyone is all riled up.** Because we want to get to a solution, we often jump in when both we and our child are still worked up from whatever conflict we want to address. It's really hard to truly listen to someone else and

understand their needs when everyone is feeling frustrated or anxious or angry!

Solution: Try to extract yourself from the immediate situation in the most delicate way possible. If your child is asking for ice cream right before bed, offer a teaspoonful. If they want more screen time, offer another five minutes. Look back to the suggestions on pages 134 and 135 to help you navigate the immediate situation, repair later, and then find ways to meet both of your needs.

7 **We try to fix an issue that isn't within the child's power to fix.** This means we need to understand what's developmentally appropriate for the child to handle. You can't tell a baby not to put things in their mouth. You can't tell a toddler not to say "no." You can't ask a preschooler to be 100 percent consistent about not hitting the baby when they're emotionally dysregulated and you're not right next to them to help.

Solution: Make sure you understand what's developmentally appropriate for your child's approximate age, as well as for your individual child. It might seem obvious to us that if you tell someone something twenty times, they should be able to remember to do it, but young children's brains aren't developed enough to be able to do that yet. Remember that a three-year-old can't stop themselves from doing something you've told them not to do unless you're right there telling them again. Even a school-aged child is likely to put their need for play above your desire to protect your belongings by putting the iPad away after they're done using it unless you remind them each time. Don't get them to agree to requests and solutions that they can't actually do in the moment. Review the list of capabilities on pages 62–63 if you need guidance on roughly what's appropriate, and if you're in doubt, assume that if the child *could* do the thing you're asking, they *would.*

8 **We expect a solution to work forever.** We had a successful Problem-Solving Conversation. We arrived at a solution that our child mostly generated and then agreed to. It works . . . for three days. Then our child refuses again, and we feel like problem-solving "doesn't work" for us.

Solution: If we can let go of the idea that a solution is forever, this one fixes itself. When the solution we jointly determine ends up not working out for one of us, that's an opportunity to have another Problem-Solving Conversation. You might start: "Hey, remember a few days ago when we agreed to do . . .? It seems like that's not really working well because I'm noticing that . . . Can we please talk about another way we can help you to [insert the child's need] while also [meeting my need]?" People's needs change over time, and once we get used to these tools, the process gets a lot faster and easier!

9 **We can't quite get over our command-and-control mindset.** In traditional parenting approaches, it's the parent's job to be in charge, to issue the commands, and to make sure the child toes the line. We might be at a point where we're thinking about giving that up, but we can't quite see what will replace it yet, and we're scared that we're giving up our control and will just end up getting walked all over.

Solution: Try to trust your child a little bit. Practice. Fail. Try again. Have some successes. This won't be easy because you're doing something new. But ultimately, it really is easier than the command-and-control model as your child will *want* to work with you because their needs are being met. Then they start to propose their own potential solutions to challenges you're both facing, which is a beautiful thing to see!

10 **The child refuses to engage.** Perhaps they shout "Don't talk to me about that!" or roll their eyes and say "I don't caaaaaaare" when you ask them how they're feeling, or they shut down and walk away. Believe me, they care. They just don't think that sharing their feelings and needs with you is going to result in any change they actually want to see.

Solution: Even if your child won't tell you how they're feeling and what their needs are, you can make a pretty good guess. A child who is refusing to engage with you is most likely feeling frustrated and probably angry as well. To understand their needs, you have to know a bit about how a child's mind works: they crave your love and attention, and also want autonomy— the ability to make decisions about what happens to them. They might hit a sibling or even you to get your attention. They don't want your negative attention, but they'd rather have that than no attention. They might stall and resist you because they don't like how something is being done, but they don't know how to tell you, or they've tried to tell you in the past, but the two of you didn't connect. Use their needs cupcake to try to hypothesize their need and then meet it to the extent you can.

PROBLEM-SOLVING THROUGH PARENTS' DIFFERING ABILITIES

It can seem like the Problem-Solving Approach works great for well-resourced parents who don't have any struggles in life—but I've also worked with parents from all kinds of backgrounds and with all kinds of challenges who still find these tools useful.

Parenting with a trauma history, mental health challenges, or a history of substance abuse

Parent Adrianna—whose two children are now problem-solving by themselves—grew up in an abusive home. She is autistic; she has obsessive-compulsive disorder and depression; and she self-medicated with alcohol, drugs, and self-harm to cope with her mental health challenges and the pain she experienced in her childhood. She has now been sober for more than eleven years but is still easily overwhelmed by loud noises and other challenges that come along with young children. Adrianna knew she needed to *not be like her parents* but had no idea what to do to make her actions match her values—while also managing her mental health. She thought power struggles, sibling squabbles, and "just surviving" were normal parts of parenting.

Now she makes sure to take time to refill her cup daily so she can show up for her children in the way she wants to. She notices when her face feels hot and her chest feels tight, and she can respond appropriately: by walking away to take a few breaths, or by saying "Hey, this is a lot for me right now; can we do something different?" After her pause, she reevaluates: Do we really have to get dressed right now? Can we slow this down? Is there a quieter thing we could do?

Stepping back from what's happening helps her to create a pause that she can use to reregulate herself and then support her children. Now her children can often work out their own solutions to problems, and even on the (now rare) occasions when they're both simultaneously having a hard time and want to be in physical contact with Adrianna, they work with her to figure out how they can do that without her feeling overwhelmed. She used to dread parenting and count down the minutes until she could take a break, and now she actually enjoys being with her children!

Parenting with ADHD

Parent Courtney deeply believes in respectful parenting because it fits so closely with her values, but having ADHD presents challenges: she is often inconsistent in setting boundaries and limits and then following through (because she gets distracted easily), and struggles with decision-making (because she can't plan in advance and then decides impulsively). She gets dysregulated easily herself, partly because of the trauma she has experienced, and often intends to have Problem-Solving Conversations with her child on issues they struggle with repeatedly but forgets to do it—although her child's self-advocacy ("I need attention!") helps her to focus on him when he needs help. She self-regulates by listening to Michael Franti songs, and when things get difficult, she tries to remember to look at sticky notes she has posted around the house to remind her of what's important: their relationship. She also finds that setting alarms helps her to follow through more effectively.

Now raising her transgender child as a single parent, they talk often about the privileges they each hold. He knows that not having a "neurotypical" brain is one of many marginalized personal characteristics, and also understands that he has less power because he is a child, compounded by being a transgender child. Courtney is keenly aware of how hurtful it is to be treated poorly because she has ADHD and is consciously using the language of feelings and needs to make sure she doesn't continue the pattern of trauma that she experienced as a child.

Their lives are more vibrant due to Courtney's neurodivergence combined with her use of the tools in this book, with amazing moments and also big expressions of difficult feelings—all said without fear of losing their love for one another, and with repair after conflicts. One of her greatest strengths is the ability to think on her feet and adapt quickly when she or her son are dysregulated to deescalate the situation without overpowering him, working to find creative ways to meet both of their needs rather than holding on to unrealistic goals and expectations. She says: "We are free to be our authentic selves, and that's exactly how I want my child to live."

Parenting with anxiety

Parent Jamie navigates both ADHD and anxiety, and when her three-year-old, Elliott, asks a question in the middle of Jamie's morning routine, she can quickly get overwhelmed and leave the house without half of the things she needs for the day. The ADHD makes it more likely she'll forget things, and mornings like this remind her that her always-simmering fear that she's forgetting something isn't unwarranted. Jamie has put in place a number of strategies to help, including:

- Trying to have her wife available to help Elliott during mornings when Jamie has to leave the house.

- Reminding herself that it's Jamie's responsibility to keep Elliott safe from having an irritated parent, which means that Jamie setting boundaries is preferable to not setting them and then exploding, even if Elliott has big feelings about the boundaries.

- Being in therapy to continue processing the sources of her childhood trauma.

Jamie has a very high degree of knowledge about child development and (anxiously) wishes she could use that knowledge to dodge every parenting pitfall. She knows this isn't realistic, but to see herself struggling at something like supporting her child in regulating her emotions is painful for her. She finds it reassuring to see what she is doing well: she doesn't abandon her child during moments of big feelings as Jamie herself was abandoned, and can recognize when their relationship needs repair. When Elliott tried to hide the fact that she had peed her pants by pretending it was water, Jamie realized they were getting into a conflict and changed the tone of the conversation by getting closer and gently saying: "I'm wondering if you peed on yourself and you're afraid of me being upset so you told me you spilled water instead?" Elliott confirmed this was true, and they had a tender and important moment in which Jamie promised to try not to say things that would make Elliott want to hide what she had done. This couldn't have happened without Jamie's "failure" (her word) in the first place, and it was an opportunity to model how their family gracefully navigates their imperfections in human relationships: through honesty, vulnerability, and the intention to honor each other's feelings.

PROBLEM-SOLVING WITH CHILDREN OF DIFFERENT AGES OR ABILITIES

I know that many parents will want detailed guidance on what kinds of problems children of different age groups will be able to engage with, and in what ways, and as tempting as it is to try to provide this, it really isn't possible because of the incredible variation in children and in our relationships with them. A middle schooler who has been coerced into meeting a parent's needs on a regular basis may essentially function at the level of a not-very-verbal three-year-old when identifying needs. A fairly verbal three-year-old whose parent has been practicing this approach for some time may be able to identify solutions that can work for both people.

For a younger child (perhaps ages two to four) or a child who has been practicing this method for only a few weeks or months, you can talk them through the process yourself: "Hmm . . . I'm seeing toys on the floor. I think you've been feeling kind of frustrated when I ask you to pick them up, right? [Hypothesizing the child's feeling and watching for acknowledgment.] I know I can feel irritated when I ask you more than once. [Sharing your feeling.] I wonder if you're not done building yet and you don't want to put your toys away until you've finished your structure? And you like building things here in the living room because then you can spend time close to us? [Hypothesizing the child's need for competence and connection; watching the child for acknowledgment.] I get it. I think I'm having a hard time with it because I don't like stepping on small toys—it hurts my feet. I also find it difficult when the toys are spread out because I feel tense when I see things on the floor that are going to need cleaning up. [Identifying your own needs for physical safety and ease.] I wonder if you would be willing to . . . [insert ideas that meet both people's needs, like confining building to the rug/a small area, putting loose parts away at the end of each day, playing with toys with lots of parts in another room, using different toys in the living room, etc.]?"

For an older child (perhaps ages four and up), you can have a frank conversation acknowledging that in the past you might have made them do things they didn't really want to do, and that whenever possible, you're going to stop doing that. If they'd be willing to share their ideas with you, you'll work with them whenever you can. It will likely take time to build up trust with them (by not forcing them into the conversations, and by not steamrolling them into solutions that meet your needs but not theirs), but when you are able to make it work, point it out! You can say: "Look! You told me what your need was, and we came up with a way to meet both of our needs!"

Some children may have needs that seem very difficult to understand—if this describes your child, they may spend a lot of time dysregulated, and you may feel like you're walking on eggshells not knowing what their next need will be, or how to anticipate it.

While many children have a fairly standard needs cupcake, with basic needs like nourishment, rest, warmth, safety, and connection as the cherry; movement/play and autonomy as the frosting; and everything else (including the right amount of sensory stimulation) in the cupcake, some children's needs are different: for example, the sensory issues become overwhelming and must be addressed before all other needs.

Some children don't like loud noises; others love them. Some aren't sensitive to clothing tags; others can't stand them. Some find pushing heavy loads around or being rolled in a heavy blanket to be regulating. If your child is often dysregulated, consider whether the amount of sensory stimulation (sight, sound, smell, touch, taste) they're getting matches their needs. Observe when they seem most dysregulated. Ask them (if they can respond). Join groups of parents whose children struggle with managing sensory input and see what they've learned. Look for patterns that can indicate an unmet need. Once you can identify and meet that need, you will likely find that the child is regulated much more often, which will help you to meet your needs for peace, ease, and collaboration.

Parenting a child with ADHD, anxiety, and sensory needs

Parent Blake has seven-year-old twins: Charlie, who presents as neurotypical, and Abigail, who has not yet been diagnosed but has shown traits consistent with ADHD, anxiety, and conflicting sensory needs. Abigail spends a lot of time in her own mental and emotional "world," where others aren't always allowed to enter. She struggles to hear and respect others' physical and emotional boundaries, and will approach and cross these many times in the process of learning them. She finds Problem-Solving Conversations difficult when she is dysregulated, and then becomes resistant to them.

Blake has identified a number of strategies to support both children. Blake will talk with Abigail separately about her feelings and needs, often in the bath, since being in water helps Abigail to stay calm and engaged in the conversation. They may also draw their conversation: Abigail loves to draw her own face and make her own marks for her feelings and body sensations. Then Blake helps both children to navigate the process of generating ideas that will meet both of their needs. They have a lot of conversations about boundaries and model using them as well: Blake makes sure that if Abigail's body language is indicating that she's not engaged in the process, they come back to the conversation later. Sometimes squeezing Blake's hands or lying on Blake's back can help Abigail to focus, as she responds well to very firm touch. Charlie is offered support in removing herself from situations that feel unsafe, and they wait until everyone is reregulated before attempting a Problem-Solving Conversation, or the situation is likely to escalate. Abigail's own boundaries are also respected as she begins to share her experience of these conversations ("I hear your voice, but it's like water washing over me. Your words aren't getting in."), and they return to the topic later. Sometimes Blake shares stories in my Parenting Membership community about Problem-Solving Conversations they've had, and other parents are in awe of the children's awareness of their own and empathy for each other's feelings and needs, and their ability to generate solutions that meet both of their needs.

Parenting a child with possible autism, anxiety, and sensory needs

Parent Maisie's six-year-old son James is currently on a wait list for a psychological evaluation; his therapist believes he may be on the autism spectrum and/or has anxiety, combined with sensory issues. Maisie describes his shoes and socks meltdowns as *"brutal."* Socks must fit exactly right and be perfectly positioned, or they "don't like" him. One of their Problem-Solving Conversations ended with flip-flops, which worked well until James's day care required shoes and socks. They eventually found a brand of socks that works, and they buy shoes a size too big so they don't rub on the sock seams—with Velcro so he can tighten them as much as he wants.

James's first day care tried to potty train him before he was really ready, which has resulted in problems with toilet training to this day. Some of these were unintentional wettings, but at times, he would walk past the bathroom to his bedroom, pull down his pants, and pee on the carpet or into the HVAC vents. A pediatric urologist and gastroenterologist told Maisie that there was nothing physically wrong with him, but Maisie had a doctor friend write an order for an X-ray, where a hard poop seven centimeters long was discovered in his rectum. They began a new journey of daily enemas and stool softener and have seen significant improvement: peeing in the bedroom has stopped completely, and about 75 percent of nights are dry.

They have problem-solved extensively on how to administer the enema, and have devised solutions to address different parts of the process. They use warm water because it's more comfortable.

James wants to feel his parents supporting him using touch. He was bored sitting on the toilet for thirty minutes; fidget spinners failed after they were dropped in the bowl too many times, but comic-style books have been a hit. James is creative and imaginative, and sometimes he and his parents do role-playing with stuffies. He has a strong sense that "things must be a certain way," so Maisie makes up ridiculous solutions to make him laugh, and then he generates

---

EXERCISE

- Establish a regular mindfulness practice. This can be as simple as picking an activity that you do multiple times a day (like making tea, looking at a certain object, or even using the bathroom), and using that time to check in with how you're doing and what you need. What would feel good right now? Perhaps a snack or a stretch or stepping outside, even if it's just for one minute?
- Plan your self-care time and activities. If you don't plan them, they're much less likely to happen. Schedule time for exercise that you enjoy, a regular conversation with a friend, or a hobby. It might seem like there isn't time, but there is—right now, this time is spent in conflict with your child. When this gets easier, it's almost like you've "created" time.
- Brainstorm self-compassion phrases. These are things you can say to yourself to remind you what's important. Examples include:

  "My relationship with my child is the most important thing."

  "There's no tiger here right now." (to remind you that whatever is happening, it probably isn't a life-or-death situation).

  "Relationships over rules."

  "They're just feelings."

---

his own ideas for solutions that fit his idea of "the right way." James also loves to draw his feelings and needs and can often find new solutions this way as well. Maisie has realized that rather than changing James so he can function in her world, she has been more successful at developing a close and positive relationship with him when she can understand his needs and then make adjustments to his world that help him navigate it better.

"I love the child I have, not the one I wish to see."

"Let go or be dragged."

"I didn't fail. I'm not weak. I will try again tomorrow."

- Make a plan for how you want to handle a stressful situation that comes up over and over again. What does your child do that annoys you? What kinds of situations lead up to it, and how can you use these to prepare yourself? So if your trigger is resisting toothbrushing, walking to the bathroom usually happens right beforehand. On your walk to the bathroom, what will you say to yourself that reminds you of your values and how you want to show up in this moment? When your child says, "I don't want to brush my teeth," what will be the first words you say?
- If you've had a difficult experience with your child recently, retell the story. Ask them if it's OK to talk about it (and don't proceed if they say "no"), and start describing what happened. Allow space for them to fill in their perspective, and work toward an apology—from you to the child, and without forcing the child to apologize to you.

CHAPTER 8:

LEVELING UP

Applying Your New Skills to the Challenges You Face

You've just learned a lot of new skills to address the problems you're having between you and your child. The awesome thing about this framework is that it can be used in *any* situation, and with *any* person (not just children)! This isn't a "trick" to convince someone to do something they don't want to or that relies on you using your power over them; it's a profoundly different way of interacting with people. But when you're new to this, it can be really hard to see how it actually applies to the specific circumstances you're facing in your own life.

In some ways, it's impossible for me to walk you through the exact situations that might come up because I don't know your needs or your child's needs. Without this information, I can't offer precise solutions that are going to get your child to do the things you want them to do (and, after all, leaving that particular idea behind is the point of this book). That's why when you read little scenarios about how to get your child to comply with you, the hypothetical children always readily agree to whatever the parent proposes, but in real life your child always goes off-script. Because the fictitious children's needs aren't the same as your real child's needs; there simply is no one solution that is guaranteed to work.

But I can help you to identify what might be *some of* your and your child's needs and, from there, some potential solutions that might meet both of your needs. There are two main categories that these situations fall within: health- and safety-related issues, and other issues. Regarding health- and safety-related issues, we're not saying that avoiding the activity is an option. If you've decided that your child will have a vaccination or a medical procedure, then we're not problem-solving whether the vaccination or procedure happens, but how to make the process meet as many of each person's needs as possible (e.g., by coming back for the vaccination on a different day if that's possible, allowing the child to use screen time while receiving the injection, etc.). If it's still simply not possible to meet the child's needs, then we're going to acknowledge that and apologize, and then proceed with the injection. Keeping a child healthy and safe overrides meeting their needs where we can't do both; we just have to be clear whether an issue is *really* health and safety related rather than telling ourselves that *all* of the limits we set are related to health and safety.

If it's not a health- or safety-related issue, then many more potential solutions are on the table, which is where things get really fun. Remember: understanding the child's needs is a critical step. If you misidentify a need, then the solutions you propose won't work because they won't meet everyone's needs.

HEALTH- AND SAFETY-RELATED ISSUES

Resistance to toothbrushing

This can be an especially challenging situation because there's no real consequence for not brushing your teeth *once*. But when each "once" adds up to *every night*, you're looking at health problems that can cost a lot of money to resolve. If your child puts up extra resistance to toothbrushing one night, let it go—for just that night—by making a graceful exit from the situation. Tell your child: "OK, I'm not going to force you to brush your teeth. Let's skip it for tonight only, and then can we talk about it tomorrow?" Then the conversation might look something like this:

NONJUDGMENTAL OBSERVATION	• "It seems like we've been having a hard time with toothbrushing lately. Can we chat about that?"
CHILD'S POSSIBLE FEELINGS	• Apprehensive (this has caused many struggles in the past and they don't want to have another one) • Helpless (they don't have any say over whether or how toothbrushing happens) • Disconnected (from you, who is trying to get the toothbrushing to happen even though the child doesn't want it) • Bored (they'd rather be playing) • Tired (it's the end of the day)
PARENT'S POSSIBLE FEELINGS	• Tired (it's the end of the day) • Exasperated (why does this have to be so hard?)

CHILD'S POSSIBLE NEEDS	• Autonomy (to make decisions about their own body) • Connectedness (with you) • Comfort (toothbrushing might hurt; the tooth-paste might not taste good) • Play (the things they enjoy doing)
PARENT'S POSSIBLE NEEDS	• Ease (to make things less of a struggle) • Collaboration (the feeling that "we're in this as a team") • Time for self-care or work (which you would be doing if you weren't having an argument over toothbrushing) • Child's health and well-being
POTENTIAL SOLUTIONS THAT MIGHT MEET BOTH PARENT'S AND CHILD'S NEEDS	• Allow the child as much choice as possible over as many aspects of the process as possible, including toothbrush style, toothpaste flavor, where in the house the teeth are brushed, etc. (which meets the need for autonomy) • Making toothbrushing more of a game (which meets the need for play and connectedness) • Use an app or other screen time for entertainment (which meets the need for play)

Refusing to get in the car seat

Obviously, if you live in a place where car seat usage is mandated by law, using the car seat isn't optional—but we can still try to make it easier.

NONJUDGMENTAL OBSERVATION	• "It seems like we've been having trouble when it's time to go in your car seat lately. Can we talk about that?"

CHILD'S POSSIBLE FEELINGS	• Uncomfortable (straps improperly positioned or too tight, incorrectly sized seat, etc.) • Bored (being in the car means not having anything to do) • Anxious (child doesn't want to go to the place you're going)
PARENT'S POSSIBLE FEELINGS	• Annoyed (at having the same struggle every day) • Embarrassed (that you're going to be late for school/work again) • Helpless (empathizing with your child's feelings but knowing the car seat is necessary)
CHILD'S POSSIBLE NEEDS	• Comfort (car seat that fits properly) • Entertainment (something interesting to do in the car) • Safety (child might be having a hard time at school, and getting into the car seat means school will follow—so a good way to identify or eliminate this as a need is to see whether resistance happens only before going to *some* destinations)
PARENT'S POSSIBLE NEEDS	• Child's safety and well-being • Cooperation (feeling like you're on the same team as your child) • Ease (moving through daily activities with a minimum amount of stress) • Efficacy (to be and be seen as a good parent and employee)
POTENTIAL SOLUTIONS THAT MIGHT MEET BOTH PARENT'S AND CHILD'S NEEDS	• Adjust the car seat, straps, and clothing to make the child comfortable • Have some special toys that are only available in the car • Address challenges the child may be having with the place you're going (day care, etc.)

Screen-time struggles

For what it's worth, here are the American Academy of Pediatrics' (AAP) current guidelines on screen time: screen time (except video chatting) for children younger than eighteen months is discouraged; children older than two should watch no more than an hour per day of high-quality programming. These guidelines are technically "research based," but the research on this topic has not shown definitively that screen time use causes poor outcomes once you take other factors like socioeconomic status into account, and the AAP seemed to revise its guidelines after it realized that nobody was actually following the recommendation for no screen time at all until a child reaches the age of two.

My personal belief is that if your family chooses to be screen free, that's fine! If your family chooses to use screens, that's fine! Know that there's no firm evidence about exactly how much screen time may be harmful to your child, so set limits based on what's suitable for your family. I have no qualms at all about using screens to keep my child occupied while I take a nap, which enables me to be a more effective parent for the rest of the day.

Also take into account that while some children may be able to regulate their own screen-time usage, this isn't the case for the vast majority of children. At the beginning of the COVID-19 shutdowns, we experimented with a month of unlimited screen time with a goal that if our then five-year-old daughter could achieve a balance of time spent on and off screens by the end of the month, we wouldn't limit her screen time after that. Toward the end of the month, we were discussing how it was going, and she said (as she was playing a game, completely unable to take her eyes off it to look at me): "I want to stop playing . . . but I can't." I don't believe it's fair to pit a developing child's brain against an industry that has invested millions—and perhaps billions—of dollars developing products that make us want to use them more. Considering your child's needs, as well as your own, can help you develop limits that they are more willing to live with—and make it easier for you to enforce them as well.

Ultimately, screen time is enormously desirable to children, and it may not be possible to fully meet both of your needs. If this is the case, try to set a limit that is reasonable to both of you and meets as many of your child's needs as possible, and then be prepared to navigate the big feelings that follow. Knowing that this limit is grounded in your values will help you to be consistent, and consistency will reduce your child's desire to test the limit repeatedly.

NONJUDGMENTAL OBSERVATION	• "It seems like we've been having a hard time at the end of screen time lately. Can we have a chat about it?"
CHILD'S POSSIBLE FEELINGS	• Resentful (that the parent is controlling something the child enjoys so much) • Angry (that they can't do the thing they enjoy) • Yearning (for more screen time)
PARENT'S POSSIBLE FEELINGS	• Afraid (that screen time is harming the child) • Self-conscious (that other people—partner, in-laws, friends, neighbors—are judging your parenting) • Anxious (that a limit is going to lead to another meltdown)
CHILD'S POSSIBLE NEEDS	• Connection (if they're gaming with friends) • Joy/entertainment (they enjoy the show/game) • Completion (to finish what they started)
PARENT'S POSSIBLE NEEDS	• Ease, collaboration (to not have the same struggle every day) • Health and safety of the child • Competence (to be and be seen as a good parent)

POTENTIAL SOLUTIONS THAT MIGHT MEET BOTH PARENT'S AND CHILD'S NEEDS	• Set a timer so the child can see how much time is remaining • Allow the child to watch to the end of whatever episode they're watching or finish their game • Provide off-screen opportunities for connection with friends • Schedule activities the child enjoys to follow screen time • Set a limit that you both agree is reasonable (note that parents often find this *much* easier after doing an unlimited screen-time experiment first, which usually demonstrates that the child cannot regulate screen time by themselves)

Sugar consumption

Many parents have a goal for their children to eat less sugar . . . and also that they will learn to regulate their own sugar intake. I've produced a number of podcast episodes on this topic so it's a bigger issue than we can fully explore here, and to some extent, it's difficult to have a true Problem-Solving Conversation about it because we may not really be open to *any* potential solution the child proposes. Some children are fairly well able to self-regulate their sugar intake; others will quite happily eat sugar all day, every day. That said, we can still make some progress.

NONJUDGMENTAL OBSERVATION	• "It seems like we have different ideas about how much sugar you eat. Would it be OK if we talk about that?"

CHILD'S POSSIBLE FEELINGS	• Irritated (that you haven't been able to see their perspective) • Longing (for delicious food) • Apprehensive (that you are about to restrict their sugar intake further)
PARENT'S POSSIBLE FEELINGS	• Afraid (that the child will suffer ill health effects) • Exasperated (that you have to argue about sugar over and over again) • On edge (if you can't find a solution that works for everyone)
CHILD'S POSSIBLE NEEDS	• Food that they find to be delicious • To be understood
PARENT'S POSSIBLE NEEDS	• Ease (not having the same argument over and over) • Clarity (knowing what's agreed to) • Safety (protection of the child's health)
POTENTIAL SOLUTIONS THAT MIGHT MEET BOTH PARENT'S AND CHILD'S NEEDS	• Agree on a reasonable amount of sweet foods (it may not be possible to truly agree on this, and some form of limit may be necessary) • Allow the child to decide what sweets are available • Allow the child to decide when sweets are eaten

ISSUES THAT AREN'T HEALTH AND SAFETY RELATED . . . BUT ARE STILL FRUSTRATING

When the issue isn't health and safety related, we may be able to consider much more creative solutions. The challenge here for the parent is to identify whether there really is a reason why the child needs to do the activity or to do it in a specific way, or whether alternate ways could also meet the parent's needs—since parents tend to be the less flexible people.

Bedtime stalling

NONJUDGMENTAL OBSERVATION	• "It seems like we've been having a hard time at bedtime lately, huh? Would it be OK if we talk about that?"
CHILD'S POSSIBLE FEELINGS	• Frazzled (it's the end of the day) • Disconnected (from you) • Excited (wound up) • Fearful (of something related to going to sleep) • Hungry
PARENT'S POSSIBLE FEELINGS	• Annoyed (that the process takes so long every night) • Dread (at knowing difficult interactions are coming) • Tired (it's the end of the day)
CHILD'S POSSIBLE NEEDS	• To get more energy out (they aren't tired yet) • Connection (with you, which is why they stall—to get more time together) • Rest/sleep (if they haven't been getting enough sleep to meet their needs) • Safety (if they are afraid of the dark) • Food
PARENT'S POSSIBLE NEEDS	• Ease, collaboration (to not have the same struggle every night) • Rest/sleep • Time for work/self-care activities

POTENTIAL SOLUTIONS THAT MIGHT MEET BOTH PARENT'S AND CHILD'S NEEDS	• Allow the child to decide when they go to bed, as long as how they're spending their time doesn't interfere with your ability to meet your needs—consider this as a potential solution from around age two • Play running-around games before bed to get excess energy out • Spend more quality time together earlier in the day so the child isn't trying to get more connection at bedtime • Schedule self-care activities that can be done while soothing the child to sleep (e.g., meditation, listening to a podcast, etc.) • Schedule self-care earlier in the day so bedtime isn't competing with these activities • Empathize with genuine fears, and install nightlights, play soft music, etc. (also look for other needs if your child says they are afraid; they may just have learned that this is a reliable strategy to get you to come back into their room when "I'm hungry!" has already failed) • Offer a tolerated-but-not-liked snack before getting ready for bed

By now, you're probably seeing something of a pattern: the parent is often feeling frustrated that they can't get the task done, and needs collaboration/cooperation, ease, and time for rest/work/self-care. So let's streamline a few more examples by just looking at hypotheses about the child's feelings and needs and potential solutions that could address these, which you'll obviously need to modify based on your own needs.

Resisting bath time

CHILD'S POSSIBLE FEELINGS	• Nervous (about being made to take a bath again) • Discomfort (doesn't like bath water in their eyes, doesn't like shampoo in their eyes, water is the wrong temperature, etc.) • Disconnected (from their preferred parent, if the other parent is giving the bath)
CHILD'S POSSIBLE NEEDS	• Comfort (with water temperature, with the feel of water on their body, with not having their eyes sting, etc.) • Connection (with the preferred parent) • Joy (making bath time fun) • Autonomy (they get to say what happens to their own body)
POTENTIAL SOLUTIONS	• Take fewer baths • Take sponge baths • Take showers instead of baths • Wash hair leaning back over a sink instead of in the bathtub • Use a visor to protect eyes from shampoo drips • Have the child wash their own hair, perhaps using squirt toys • Let the child set the water temperature • Have the preferred parent do bath time for a while • Have the preferred parent spend ten minutes with the child before bath time • Bring favored (waterproof!) toys into the bath • Bring new toys in the bath (e.g., kitchen equipment)

Dropping food or the plate off the dinner table

CHILD'S POSSIBLE FEELINGS	• Boredom (not wanting to sit at the table any longer) • Curiosity (wanting to see what you do when they drop food) • Amused (at what happens to the food; at your reaction)
CHILD'S POSSIBLE NEEDS	• Joy/play • Challenge • Exploration • Connection (with you)
POTENTIAL SOLUTIONS	• Give smaller portions of food • Don't use a plate; put food straight on the tray/ table • Remove the food/plate as soon as the child is done eating and let them leave the table • Focus attention on the child during mealtime; you eat at a different time

Violent behavior (hitting, biting, kicking, etc.)

A reframe can be helpful here; instead of problem-solving "how to get the child to stop hitting" (which the child already knows they aren't supposed to do, even if they can't stop themselves), we can work to identify and meet the unmet needs that are causing them to hit. The more the hitting seems to occur randomly, unrelated to a specific type of incident, the more you should consider macro-scale causes of dysregulation like chronic lack of sleep, need for more connection a big life event (e.g., birth of a sibling, house move, job change), unhappiness in day care/school, etc. You can try identifying strategies to use in dysregulated moments, but the child will probably not be able to remember to use the strategies. It's much more effective to understand the unmet needs that are causing the dysregulated behavior and address them earlier in the cycle, not when the child is hitting.

CHILD'S POSSIBLE FEELINGS	There could be a variety of options, including: • Disconnected (from parent) • Anxious (e.g., about an upcoming situation/procedure, or about going to day care/preschool) • Jealous (e.g., toward a sibling) • Impatient • Frustrated • Embarrassed • Ashamed • Tired • Hurt Note that sometimes a child will laugh after hitting, biting, or kicking, but this doesn't indicate feeling happy—it's more of an anxious reaction.
CHILD'S POSSIBLE NEEDS	Again, there may be a huge variety depending on the situation, such as: • Acceptance • Affection • To be understood • Safety • Movement • Autonomy • Space
POTENTIAL SOLUTIONS	This will vary based on the need identified; the important part is that we aren't problem-solving "how to get the child to stop hitting" but what need they are trying to express through hitting.

Refusing to help tidy up

This is a tricky one because it has a lot to do with how we see chores in Eurocentric cultures—as something uninteresting to be done as fast as possible so we can spend time doing things that are fun. The most effective strategies here are likely to include: involving children in household chores from an early age, even when their "help" isn't actually very helpful; and doing chores as a team rather than sending them to their room to clean up while you do a different chore.

CHILD'S POSSIBLE FEELINGS	• Annoyed (that they can't keep playing) • Bored (they've learned that chores aren't interesting) • Disconnected (from you, if you're doing different chores in a different room) • Confused (if they don't know how to do the chore—"put things where they belong" might seem like a simple instruction to you, but it can be overwhelming to a child)
CHILD'S POSSIBLE NEEDS	• Joy/play • Connection • Competence
POTENTIAL SOLUTIONS	• Make tidying up fun—turn on music and have a dance party • Tidy one area together, then move on to another area together instead of splitting up • Provide more precise instruction on what you want done ("Can you put the scissors in the top drawer?") • Look for other chores the child is willing to help with if you agree to do the tidying

There are times, though, when a child just isn't motivated to help. In this case, I find these strategies useful:

- Having fewer toys out so even if the child doesn't help clean up, I can do it myself without feeling resentful.

- When my child initially refuses to help, I say: "I'm happy to help this time, and tomorrow I hope you'll be willing to help." This indicates that I'm not going to fall on my sword over this issue and also sets the expectation that I'm not going to keep doing it forever (note the "and" instead of the "but" as well).

- If the child refuses again the next day, I do the task for them without comment, and then wait a few minutes until they invariably need my help. At that point, I get down on their level and say in a kind (not accusatory) tone: "I asked you for help a few minutes ago, and you refused. Now you're asking me for help. *I'm going to help you*, and I *want* to help you much more when you help me. Our family works much better when we all help each other out. Now, what was it you needed?"

The key here is that we're working to meet our needs and our child's needs, and we're doing it in a way that doesn't assume our way is the right one. If the child is chronically refusing to help, consider that they might be feeling very disconnected from you, in which case, *that's* the challenge to address rather than specifically the issue of not helping.

ADMITTING THAT WE DON'T HAVE ALL THE ANSWERS

The monumental shift we're making by doing this work is that we're starting to wonder: *Am I always right?* When we talk with our friends about parenting, we may even be the first to admit that we have no idea what the hell we're doing, but when we're with our child, we somehow think that we have to project supreme confidence at all times because if we don't, our child will see through us and they'll push us until they can get away with anything.

The thought of confessing to our child that we don't know what we're doing might seem impossible right now. But if we can open our relationship with our child up to the possibility that we actually don't know everything, that we don't know the best way of doing things, that we often are stuck in our ways for no reason other than that way worked for us a long time ago (or our parents made us do it like that), we open up a whole host of options in our relationship.

We're all creatures of habit. When we're approaching any problem from the perspective of "how do I get my child to . . . ," we're assuming that our way is the only way. Because our children don't have the decades of patterns we've laid down in doing this activity, they're more able to see when doing it doesn't meet their needs. They resist, and we think the easiest path (which was laid down for us by our parents) is that we need to get them to see things our way. We think that once the child sees the superior logic in our perspective, they'll be persuaded that our way is indeed the right way.

But so often, it isn't! It's just something we've fallen into the habit of doing, and there are many other ways of doing these things (or even not doing them!) that could better meet everyone's needs. What follows are just a few examples from me and other parents I work with.

When my daughter was three, she went through a phase of not wanting to brush her teeth. My need was to protect her health and well-being; her need was for autonomy over a process when I wasn't giving her a choice about whether or not it happened. Her proposed solution: brush teeth in the living room (with fluoride-free toothpaste, so she didn't have to spit). She cheerfully brushed her teeth there for several months before we transitioned back to the bathroom.

Parent Megan explained: "We slept with our daughter because she breastfed and didn't sleep well as an infant. When she was three and still co-sleeping, we were over it. (Need for rest and sexual expression.) We bought her a new bed and bedding set. She went to sleep in her room most nights but often still wandered into our bed by midnight. Finally we asked: 'What should we do to help you sleep in your room all night?' The answer: 'Paint the walls pink with white polka dots, the ceiling purple, and put up some glow-in-the-dark stars.' 'Done, kid.' And she has slept in her room every night ever since." The child's needs were for autonomy over the transition process and safety/security (the stars have a comforting low-light effect she likes).

Parent Milda shared: "We live in a country where it's *very* cold in the winter, and I don't want my daughter to get sick (need to protect the child's safety), and she does not want to get dressed in the morning because she doesn't like the clothes I pick out (need for autonomy). I was so tired of fighting her over this! (Need for a sense of ease and collaboration.) One morning, I said to her: 'I hear you want to have more of a say over what you wear. You can wear whatever you like, and it's fine with me.' And the child . . . went and got dressed! In weather-appropriate winter clothes!" (Note that this kind of response doesn't always happen, but genuinely trying to meet the child's need almost always loosens something up and makes them want to collaborate with us a bit more instead of resisting.)

WHERE WE'RE HEADED IN THE LONG TERM

Teenagers will commonly say to each other: "My parents just have no idea." Think back to your own teenage years: Did you tell your parents about things that were important to you, or did you hide these so they wouldn't find out? Did you know they would try to understand your needs even if they felt angry, or did you know there would be consequences for your misbehavior? Did you trust them to hold your needs with just as much care and reverence as their own?

When we move toward using the Problem-Solving Approach with our children in this way, we're doing three things:

1 We're finding solutions to the challenges we face with our children right now.

2 We're showing them (not just telling them) what it means to live with deep respect for ourselves and also treat other people in the same way. We learn to stop lying continually to ourselves and others ("I'm fine." "Thanks, I loved the gift." "I didn't do it; it wasn't me." "I don't care whether we visit your parents or mine for the holidays.") and instead say what we really think and how we really feel. We learn how to say "no," and to hear "no" as "That doesn't meet my need right now" rather than as a rejection of us. Social norms (mostly with other adults!) can make this difficult in the beginning, especially if we've been hiding what we really think and feel from them for a long time. Just like saying "penis" and "vulva" when talking about our children's anatomy rather than "privates" or "pee-pee" and "cookie jar," it gets easier the more you practice.

3 We're increasing the likelihood that our children will go out into the world seeing and treating others with deep respect. And when that happens, I believe we'll be in a much better place to address challenges like White supremacy, patriarchy, and capitalism—and all the issues that stem from these, like poverty; homelessness; poor labor conditions; mistreatment of BIPOC people, youth, and the elderly; and environmental harms, to name but a few.

WE'RE ALL IN THIS TOGETHER

Building Your Village

There's a tendency in the self-help industry in general, and in parenting books in particular, to focus only on you (and your child). If things aren't going well for you, then it's your fault and thus your responsibility to fix whatever flaw in yourself is causing the problem you're having. There's no acknowledgment that the problem you're having might be because social expectations (being the perfect parent and doing it all by yourself) are completely unrealistic—and that it's these expectations, and not you, that need to be fixed.

It's tragic that we're likely to need community the most at the very moment when we have the least bandwidth to create it. But this is where we are, and while creating community does take work, you may well find that doing this helps you to meet needs that haven't been met for you in a long time (like collaboration, relaxation, and being known/understood). Not having community can put us in a place where we don't feel as though we have the time and energy to learn a new way of interacting with our children like we've covered in this book. So rebuilding our communities—while also taking time and energy—can ultimately create more of both. We create capacity by taking care of ourselves and by being in relationship with others.

Gender nonbinary activist Alok says that "my power is in community . . . in relinquishing power you get to be vulnerable, which creates community." White supremacy and patriarchy teach us that being vulnerable is simply too scary to be possible, so we have to pay for the services that we would otherwise freely exchange. To break these systems down, we have to be willing to be a little bit vulnerable and to share our full true selves, rather than only the sanitized parts. It is through recognizing the parts that we've suppressed, and healing and nurturing these, and finding communities that honor and respect them, that we truly create our village.

The process of learning about topics like White supremacy, patriarchy, and capitalism can be extraordinarily painful, because we've been socialized to accept them our entire lives. (And the closer we are to the White, cisgender, heterosexual, male norm, the more difficult it is to accept that what we've learned so far in our lives might not be entirely correct.) I remember when I first started learning about my White privilege as a parent, which was something I had absolutely no idea existed until that point. I felt horribly embarrassed that I hadn't seen it before now, especially since I thought I knew about systemic racism. I felt guilty that I'd benefited from this unearned advantage, frustrated that my "knowledge" had been so inaccurate, and excited—as if I'd stumbled onto the edge of some great secret, and that there was so much more to know than the narrow world I'd experienced so far. It also felt very scary to be taking this journey in public (via podcast episodes) and to know that systems that had been set up for me to succeed were actually hurting other people. By far the easiest path would have been to shut it down and disengage from the topic.

My growth on these issues happened partly through reading and learning, but my strength comes from communities: early on, my friend Amy (who has been out in front on these topics for years now) taught me how to balance knowing that I have important work to do with the knowledge that, however much I personally do, it will never be enough. Through my friend Brian Stout's Building Belonging community, I learned about the connections between White supremacy, patriarchy, and capitalism. In a book club discussion on Resmaa Menakem's *My Grandmother's Hands*, I started to learn how to be in relationship with Black people in a way that owns my role and truth and holds space for their role and truth as well—using the tools presented in this book.

It hasn't been a linear journey (there has been lots of discouragement along the way), and I've learned as I've gone along about the importance of paying attention to my body's signals in this area as well. On this topic, these signals can sometimes lead me astray: we're conditioned to accept Whiteness, patriarchal power, and capitalism as the norm, so it may feel safest to stay within these systems if they have protected us thus far. It can be difficult to move *toward* the unease, tightness, and confusion ("Am I doing this right or am I completely messing up?") associated with breaking out of them, but over time, it does get easier. This is one reason why most of this book focuses on shifting the ways of being in relationship with people in our own families—it can feel like a more approachable place to start.

Just addressing this topic from a cognitive perspective ("racism is wrong") doesn't get me to where I want to go. I need to take on these ideas and know them deeply in my body as well. It's not a journey I'll ever finish, even though I must eventually stop editing this book and put it out into the world, drawing a line in the sand to say: "This is where I am right now."

I recognize that my own journey here (and yours too) is only part of the point. This isn't only work that I (or you) can do by my(your)self. We can't read the right books, think about the right things, and magically our White supremacist, patriarchal, capitalist society will be healed. We also have to be in relationships with others in a way that honors our values to the extent that we can in our current system.

HOW TO FIND COMMUNITY

I think one reason we struggle to find communities that resonate is that we hope and expect to find one group of people that fulfills all functions for us. We want the people we hang out with to have children that our children like. We want the parents to interact with their children in the same ways that we would interact with ours, and we also want the parents to be interested in the same things that interest us.

It's a lot to ask! Inherent in this issue is the idea that someone with a voice different from our own couldn't really be "our people," when actually we might be able to find "our people" in a variety of different forms. Recognizing that "our people" doesn't have to be one or a few people who check *all* the boxes, but that there could be many people who each check a box or two, frees us up to stop looking for perfection and to find community much closer to home.

Building on the work of Black writers (e.g., bell hooks, Mia Birdsong, adrienne maree brown) as well as my own research and experience, I offer a few ideas to help you build your own village. There's no magic formula here; I can't promise you that if you follow all these steps in the right order like a recipe that you'll get your perfect community at the end. Not all of these steps are even needed: you could try whichever seems most approachable to you and keep adding more steps until your need for connection feels fulfilled.

1 **Start an emergency contact list for your street.** This gives you
a great excuse to meet everyone! Our neighbor put a note
in everyone's mailbox asking them to provide them with
names, phone numbers, email addresses, names of children in
the house, emergency contacts, pets' names, locations of gas
shutoff valves, and medical or dietary needs useful in case of
an emergency. Once you have everyone's contact info, you can
start a listserv to communicate about neighborhood events and
concerns.

2 **Introduce yourself to people you meet.** This is easiest when
someone moves into the neighborhood, when it isn't awkward
that you don't know each other—bringing a small gift may be
appreciated. If you have neighbors to whom you've somehow
never introduced yourself, you could say hi when you pass
them on the street: "Hey, you live here, right? We're just up the
street, and somehow we've never met! I'm Jen . . ." Build routines around things you enjoy: sit out on your stoop, visit your
local coffee shop at the same time every day, go to story time at
the library. When your child is playing with another child at the
park, introduce yourself to the parent or caregiver.

3 **Involve your child in these relationships.** When you're chatting
with people, try to have your children around. If you do a favor
for a neighbor, have your child help as well. If they have a child,
let your child play with theirs while you're chatting with the
adults. When everyone feels comfortable, you may end up in a
situation where the children drift from one home to the next as
they play.

4 **Ask for help.** When you need support, reach out to a friend or neighbor. This could be as simple as asking a neighbor to bring your trash cans out to the curb if you're away for a few days, or a recommendation for someone to provide a service you need. For friends you know better, reach out when you're having a tough week and need dinner made. Ask others for help with childcare—when you're running to the grocery store and your child doesn't want to go or when you just need thirty minutes to yourself because you think you might actually crack. When we ask for help, others are more likely to accept help when we offer it: then we have the start of a real relationship.

5 **Offer help.** When you see someone who needs support, offer help. If someone's going away, offer to keep an eye on their house. If you know of major life changes that are happening to your friends or neighbors, check in with them. Bring food. Send them a note making it clear that while you won't butt in where you're not wanted, you hope they'll reach out. Offer to take their child for an afternoon so everyone can get a break.

Look out for people who might be struggling financially in a way that's impacting their children. Rather than reporting this to the authorities (who may separate family members), get to know the family. It's through having a genuine relationship with the family where each of you makes meaningful contributions that you can offer support that isn't White saviorism, as you'll see the things they need that you might be able to provide. Then if you think that an offer of help could be useful and welcomed, it becomes a small aspect of your relationship rather than the main feature of it. Don't keep tabs on who offers help to whom, and don't accept money or other favors in exchange. This is how you'll build a truly reciprocal relationship.

6 **Have real conversations, and listen deeply.** When we meet new people, especially new parents, it's easy to slip into a conversation about children—as if *our children* are the most interesting thing about us. I often like to start conversations with people I just met with the question: "So, what are you passionate about?" That opens up the opportunity for the person to share about their children (if that really is their passion), or a job (if they have one, but the question doesn't assume they do and so doesn't shame a person who doesn't), or a skill or hobby, or a cause they believe in.

When they're talking, listen deeply. Pay attention only to them. Be vulnerable. When they're listening to you, watch for these signals, which indicate that you may have found a kindred spirit. Be aware that not everyone wants to enter into this kind of relationship with you, and respect that preference if needed.

7 **Be in communities linked to things you care about (or create them if they don't exist yet).** Develop relationships with people around your talents, skills, and/or interests. My daughter and I love spending time in the outdoors. A few years ago I sent out an email to just seven family friends, explaining that I knew they all had young children, I wanted to spend time outside with them, and asking if they'd like to be on a list of people I email once a month about an outdoor activity. This list has now blossomed to about thirty families. It's become a beautiful way for people to share a common interest and also talk about things other than children (since the children usually keep themselves fairly well engaged in the mud!).

8   **Understand what your resources are, and look for opportunities to share them.** Join a reparations group online and share finan-cial resources, the ability to write letters to authority figures, tutoring, business advice, and other skills you have. I have the platform of a podcast (and now a book!), and I use these to share messages about these issues. Other people have far more skills than I do in things like consensus building, website devel-opment, photography, and so on. Each of these skills can be used to support BIPOC-led groups who often lack the financial resources to do all the work they'd like to do.

9   **Practice mutual aid and direct political action based on it.** I learned about the idea of mutual aid from Dean Spade, who wrote a great book about it. Pick an issue you care about and where you have resources to help and join a mutual aid group (find a partial listing at https://www.mutualaidhub.org) to offer help to others. Or if you need help, look for it in a mutual aid group. Unlike many nonprofits, these groups offer support to everyone who needs it, regardless of their circumstances (e.g., addiction, previous incarceration, being unhoused), see the challenges people are facing as symptoms of a broken system rather than as individual failings, and recognize that *all* people have strengths. When you are in genuine relationships with people who share common interests, you're more likely to together come up with creative ideas to take direct action against obstacles that prevent *everyone* from thriving.

10 **If you're White, be in community with people who aren't like you.** When I talked with Akilah Richards about what White people who have power within the system of White supremacy, and who are also repressed within it, can do to make sure we're not

causing more harm as we're working to dismantle the system, her answer was simple: be in community with Black women.

11 **Be in community over food.** Community organizer Sita Kuratomi Bhaumik describes in Mia Birdsong's book *How We Show Up* that cooking and eating together are key parts of building community. When we work together to prepare food, we aren't hiding the food's origins to serve a finished product to a customer. We can be more aware of the land the food was grown on, the people whose hands brought it to us, and the labor it took to transform it into a meal. There's a reason many families bond over marathon tamale-, pasta-, and dumpling-making sessions: the repetitive actions create space for us to have real conversations so both the cooking and the conversations become a full-bodied experience. Being in community with others is a lot different from being served by others.

12 **White readers: before you're in community with BIPOC people, do your own learning.** Read books about antiracist work. Talk about it in your communities. But if your actions stop at having a book club, know that there's lots more to be done. What are the ways that White supremacy, patriarchy, and capitalism show up in your family, communities, and work? What steps can you take to begin dismantling these systems? Yes, this work is hard. It's uncomfortable. It requires growth and change and vulnerability. And it's worth it.

13 **Check for an (orgasmic) yes.** This one comes straight from adrienne maree brown's book *Pleasure Activism*: "I began to make decisions about whether I wanted to do things in my life and in the movements I am part of by checking for my orgasmic

yes. And to feel for resistance inside, the small place in my gut that knows before I do that something is not a fit for me and will not increase my aliveness." The same check-ins we do with our body to sense when something isn't right for us (because our need isn't being met) can also be used to sense what we want to move *toward*. Check for a sense of expansiveness, lightness, drawing toward, connection, and joy about ideas you believe to be right—even if it can feel a bit scary to reveal parts of yourself that you had previously hidden. Move toward people and experiences that accept you for who you are, and allow for your growth. As Dr. Carol Gilligan and Naomi Snider say so poignantly: "I felt again the exquisite freedom and pleasure of being myself in relationship. Why, for all the riches in the world, would I give this up?" We can't live vicariously through our partner's and children's experiences and achievements, expecting that our needs will be met by them *after* theirs are met. Our needs are just as valid, and can be met *alongside* their needs.

Dismantling patriarchy, capitalism, and systemic racism isn't only work to be done by parents, and it isn't only work to be done in families. We must also do it in our workplaces, in our churches, and among our friends, and we must do it with people who aren't parents as well. When we do it in our families, we make parenting so much easier today—and we establish the kinds of relationships we want to have with our children for the rest of our lives. We're also much more likely to raise the kind of adults who will be in genuinely respect-based relationships with other people as they move through their lives—which is exactly the quality we need to heal not just our families, but our culture and the world.

SUMMARY OF KEY IDEAS

I know we've covered a lot of ground in this book. We took two ideas that may have seemed completely unrelated—the challenges we're having with our child's behavior and the social problems we see out in the world—and saw how they're intimately related.

We also learned some new tools that will address both of these challenges. I understand that these can feel a bit "clunky" when you first start using them. As Oren Jay Sofer says in his book *Say What You Mean*, the tools aren't the point. Connection is the point. If the tools get in the way of connecting, then don't use them. But the more we practice them, the more they become second nature. Even if your partner isn't on board with all this "feel-good nonsense," they're likely to become interested when your children stop having tantrums when they're with you.

Pretty soon you will get to a point when your children start bringing ideas to you that meet both of your needs—and do this with each other as well. Then you're no longer the referee of their (many!) daily arguments because they can understand each other's needs and find solutions that meet both of their needs.

NEED A CHEAT SHEET? HERE IT IS:

- White supremacy, patriarchy, and capitalism are the most important forces that shape our society.

- Our parents, who wanted us to be successful in a world shaped by these forces, constrained our behavior so we would "fit in." They taught us to hide parts of ourselves that weren't socially acceptable as a condition of belonging in the family.

- We have experienced extensive consequences of our parents' denial of our needs, which caused us to deny our own needs and then forget that we even have needs. We have a sense of loss—of parts of ourselves, of a village that can nurture us, and of truly being known by others. We use unskillful strategies to try to make ourselves feel better, like blaming others when we feel hurt and trying to get them to change their behavior.

- Our children resist us because they have needs too, and they haven't yet learned not to make these known. If we don't consciously decide to do something differently, we are likely to repeat the same parenting patterns that our own parents modeled for us—through rewarding and punishing our children into doing what we want them to do.

- When we can hold their needs with curiosity and as much care as we hold our own needs, we can find ways to meet both of our needs in the vast majority of situations. We can do this by:
  » Making a nonjudgmental observation about the challenge we're having together.
  » Understanding each person's feelings and creating empathy for each other's struggles.
  » Uncovering each person's needs (which are different from the strategies we use to meet our needs), which enables us to find solutions that work for both of us.
  » Making a request of the other person to help us meet our needs and offering ideas to help them meet their needs as well.

In the few situations when we can't meet both people's needs, we can use (in order of preference):

When the major consequence affects the child

> » Natural consequences (things that happen without us making a decision).
> » Logical consequences (the lightest punishment possible; tightly related to the task at hand; more likely to rupture the relationship).

When the major consequence affects the parent

> » Boundaries ("I am not willing to . . ."; can only be used when we control whether we take an action).
> » Limits ("You may not . . .; appropriate when the child's behavior cannot be tolerated for health or safety reasons; more likely to rupture the relationship).

- When we use these tools, we:
  > » Heal ourselves, because we understand our own needs and get these met more often.
  > » Show our children that they can be their full selves, and that we will love them as their full selves.
  > » Be in family relationships where each person gets their needs met.
  > » Begin to heal our culture, as we use these tools with others in the wider world, with a deep sense of respect for others' needs and a genuine desire to meet their needs as well as ours.

- We don't have to use these tools perfectly. Often the process of trying to see the other person's needs loosens something up in the interaction and makes them willing to come toward us even if we aren't able to find a solution that truly works for everyone. Beating ourselves up because we "can't do it" doesn't help; it just digs us deeper into a hole. Being willing to try, fail, and try again models this valuable life skill for our children.

ACKNOWLEDGMENTS

This book was conceived—like some children—by accident. When I heard on fellow podcaster and friend Malaika Dower's now (sadly) defunct podcast *How to Get Away with Parenting* that parents of Black children can't take them into a grocery store with their own food because someone might think they stole it, and that they fear allowing a Black boy to have a tantrum in a public place because White people are so terrified of out-of-control Black boys, I suddenly realized that I have White privilege as a parent—something I'd never had cause to consider before. When I asked Malaika how I might approach a podcast episode on the trauma that Black families have suffered as a result of prejudice and racism, she kindly redirected me to instead look at the role of Whiteness in my life, which launched a series of episodes on the intersection of race and parenting.

Amy Law and Brian Stout helped the embryo to implant by offering support and intellectual stimulation at critical moments in those early days; seeing them out in front of me gave me the confidence to continue on my own journey.

The *Your Parenting Mojo* listener and member community deserve special thanks for nurturing both me and these ideas. Some people don't like that I reflect on the biases inherent in the culture that the (supposedly objective) scientific research sits within. Thanks to those listeners who write that they do appreciate this, like thedreadpirater-oberts17, who gave a five-star iTunes review before they even started listening because of other reviewers' warnings of a "clear liberal and feminist bias." Guilty as charged!

Parents in my Parenting Membership gave me space to develop and test my ideas, using research as a starting point and also going far beyond it. Special thanks to Anne Hamlin, Denise Suarez, iris Padela-Hunter, Jamie Ramirez, Kathryn Dent, Katie Stanke, Kesha Jones, Lucinda Woodward, Madeline Thompson, Milda Rosenberg, Miranda Fleming, Nicole Glazebrook, and Sarah O'Flaherty.

Thanks to the *Your Parenting Mojo* team (and especially to Lori Ann) who work on the parts of running the business that I'm not good at.

Elizabeth Hollis Hansen at New Harbinger saw the potential for a book in my work, but it turned out to be Braxton-Hicks contractions rather than the actual birth.

Hannah and Kelty of Upbringing taught me lessons about openness, generosity, and collaboration through our work together as well as through their introduction to editor Hannah Elnan at Sasquatch Books. I so appreciate you both—as well as Dana Schmidt for connecting us in the first place.

Sarah Hinman held me through a difficult transition when it seemed like I was drowning in the vomit (why does nobody tell you that you might throw up during labor?). I know it felt like you weren't doing anything. You did everything.

Hannah Elnan was this book's doula: from our very first interaction, I knew you "got" the book as I learned how to transform it from being a manifesto into a guide to really help parents. Thanks also to Isabella Hardie and Anna Goldstein at Sasquatch for designing and shepherding the book into reality.

Heather Patterson and Matt Zimmerman generously provided their cabin in McCall, Idaho, so that I could begin to birth the first draft at just the right time. I spent two weeks almost entirely alone, but the members of CMarie Fuhrman's Tuesday Writers Group at the McCall Public Library inspired me to stop putting off writing what became the Preface and Chapter 1.

My listener community really stepped up to make the writing process a collaborative one, from offering ideas and advice, to helping me "illustrate" the book through their stories and reading early drafts. In addition to those mentioned already, thanks to Adrianna M., Alex, Amy M., Caroline B., Cassie, Claire B., Courtney C., Dana O., Elizabeth M., Ginelle C., Jamie R., J. D., Kelly P., Kelsey B., Kim R., Liann J., Lulu L., Maisie, Maria, Masako, Megan E., Melissa P., Nicole C., Rebecca C., Sara G., Sarah Z., Shira F., Skarlet K., Stephanie D., and Winnie (some of these names are pseudonyms). Because of you, this book resonates with real experiences.

Early readers Erin Rance, Salisha Old Bull, and May Ermyas helped to make the book more inclusive and relevant to all readers; any remaining missteps are my own responsibility.

Thanks to Alvin, who has stuck with me through it all. A few years ago, I read Ruth Bader Ginsburg's obituary in the *New York Times*, which contained a paragraph that made it so clear how proud her husband, Martin, was of her. For half a second, I wondered what it would be like to have someone be that proud of me, and then I realized I already knew. (Although perhaps not *everyone* on social media needs to know it too . . .)

And thanks, of course, to Carys—even though you were unimpressed when you learned I was going to write a book until I told you that you would be in it. Right after you were born, my primary concern was figuring out how I was still going to hike with an infant (turned out that wasn't such a problem!). But I had no idea how much you were going to permeate every aspect of my life and, by extension, this book. I love the relationship we have now, and I'm so glad that I get to grow alongside you.

RESOURCES

The following short list is intended to help you dive a little deeper into the topics of White supremacy, patriarchy, and capitalism. Resources indicated by an asterisk have one or more authors who identify as BIPOC.

ADDRESSING WHITE SUPREMACY/RACISM

Radical Belonging by Lindo Bacon
Their most recent book connects White-supremacist-based body-size issues with broader ideas of belonging. Delve into their older books for a debunking of ideas on body size and health.

*Social Justice Parenting by Dr. Traci Baxley
This is a good place to start for parents who are new to social-justice-oriented parenting (although we do have different approaches to household rules).

The Politics of Trauma by Staci K. Haines
Breaking down the brain/body divide to understand the wisdom in our bodies—and be in right relationship with our communities.

*Raising Antiracist Children by Britt Hawthorne
A beyond-the-basics book on having conversations about racism and taking antiracist actions with your children.

*Rest Is Resistance: A Manifesto by Tricia Hersey
Hersey argues that we should rest in service of ourselves as we work toward dismantling White supremacy.

*How to Be an Antiracist by Ibram X. Kendi
A memoir of and guide for a journey to become an antiracist.

*How to Raise an Antiracist by Ibram X. Kendi
A review of the literature on children and racism, told through the lens of the author's child's life.

*Decolonizing Non-Violent Communication by Meenadchi
This tiny book will help to integrate often overlooked body-based practices into Problem-Solving Conversations (Non-Violent Communication).

*My Grandmother's Hands by Resmaa Menakem
A book that's worth reading and rereading on how racial trauma lives in the body—and how to heal from it.

*Set Boundaries, Find Peace by Nedra Glover Tawwab
White supremacy creates boundaries between us and the outside world, and tells us we can't have boundaries between family members. Learn how to set and hold them with this book.

*Parenting Decolonized podcast hosted by Yolanda Williams
Run by a Black parent for Black parents; all parents will get something from listening.

ADDRESSING PATRIARCHY

***Feminism for the 99%: A Manifesto by Cinzia Arruzza,
Tithi Bhattacharya, and Nancy Fraser**
This compelling book argues that feminism needs to be relevant to all people's concerns, not just those of wealthy White women, and that effective feminism is also antiracist and anti-capitalist.

Man Enough by Justin Baldoni
Understanding the harms of patriarchy from the inside—by someone who should be a primary beneficiary—from an engaging, humble author.

Why Does Patriarchy Persist? by Carol Gilligan and Naomi Snider
Gilligan has been writing on patriarchy for decades. This conversational book connects patriarchy with attachment theory.

*The Will to Change: Men, Masculinity, and Love by bell hooks
A Black feminist classic; this is a damning indictment of the effects
of patriarchy on families and our culture, and how to begin healing.

Spinning Threads of Radical Aliveness by Miki Kashtan
Long but immensely readable, this is a distillation of Kashtan's
wisdom for those wanting to dive deeply.

For the Love of Men by Liz Plank
A useful collection of research and ideas on patriarchy—which isn't
just about hating men.

ADDRESSING CAPITALISM

Sacred Economics, Revised by Charles Eisenstein
An insightful work on how we transform "free" resources into
things for sale so we can pay back the debt that is created through
money—and turn life into a competition to get more money.
Available on a gift-economy basis at Sacred-Economics.com!

Debt: The First 5,000 Years by David Graeber
Lengthy yet readable, this book connects the dots from the origins
of debt through to its effect on our society today. It has been criticized by right-wing economists as being an unlikely explanation for
the origins of debt.

Wanting What's Best by Sarah W. Jaffe
This guide shows how the decisions that financially (and racially)
privileged families make affect all families, and offers real suggestions for places to start dismantling that privilege.

Doughnut Economics by Kate Raworth
Raworth provides ideas for how we can reform capitalism to make
it serve people more effectively. I believe capitalism cannot be effectively overhauled because it is designed to create inequality, but this
gives us stopgap tools while we figure out alternatives.

ACTIONS TO TAKE

To Heal From and Dismantle White Supremacy, Patriarchy, and Capitalism in Our Society

---

Any two-page list of actions is going to be necessarily incomplete; these are intended to be some ideas to get you started.

1   Practice the Problem-Solving Approach described in this book with your children, which helps them to be whole people who are seen, respected, and accepted by the person they love most.

2   Put these practices into place with other people in your life as well (partners, parents, colleagues, employees).

3   Ask yourself: Why do we do things this way? Have we just assumed that this is the best way to do it when other ways are equally valid? Have we assumed that we are the only person who can take on this chore? Female-identifying parents often take on the lion's share of the household work, and this does not have to be the case.

4   Acknowledge that who does the chores is only half of what matters in disrupting patriarchal systems—the other half is who holds the power to decide who does the chores. Consider exerting your power if you are doing more than half of the chores.

5 Change whose views you see. Follow Black thinkers and writers on social media. Read their books. Don't expect a single answer to the question: What should I do? But try to take actions that resonate with your values that BIPOC people have asked you to take.

6 Be in community with others, whether this is over food, over drinks in someone's driveway on a Friday afternoon, or in a park. Share what's (really) going on in your world and find out how you can support others. Mia Birdsong's book *How We Show Up* has great ideas to get started. Akilah Richards reminds us to do antiracist work by being in community with Black women.

7 If you identify as White or as a person with racial privilege, take the time to learn about how your privilege affects how you show up in the world. Don't be a Nice White Parent. Work to reduce the impact of privilege by equalizing differences in resources, and stand up for those who have fewer resources than you do. Fight for resources for all children in school, not just resources that will benefit your child.

8 Buy less stuff . . . for yourself, for your children. Reuse. Repair. Share. Wherever you can, substitute relationships for payment.

LIST OF FEELINGS WHEN NEEDS <u>ARE</u> MET

This is an inexhaustive list designed to increase your fluency with talking about feelings, without getting hung up on identifying *precisely* the right word. Rather than organize the lists alphabetically, I've arranged them roughly from less intense to more intense feelings within each subheading to help you more quickly land on the word that expresses the intensity of your feeling.

AFFECTIONATE
Friendly
Openhearted
Tender
Warm
Loving
Compassionate

ENGAGED
Alert
Curious
Absorbed

HOPEFUL
Encouraged
Optimistic

CONFIDENT
Open
Safe
Proud
Empowered

EXCITED
Surprised
Energetic
Enthusiastic
Invigorated
Passionate
Vibrant

GRATEFUL
Appreciative
Thankful
Touched

INSPIRED
Wonder
Awed

JOYFUL
Happy
Pleased
Amused
Glad
Jubilant

EXHILARATED
Elated
Enthralled
Radiant
Thrilled

PEACEFUL
Calm
Clearheaded
Comfortable
Centered
Content
Fulfilled
Relaxed
Relieved
Satisfied

REFRESHED
Rested
Renewed
Enlivened

LIST OF FEELINGS WHEN NEEDS ARE <u>NOT</u> MET

CONFUSED
Hesitant
Ambivalent
Bewildered
Lost

DISCONNECTED
Distracted
Bored
Cold
Indifferent
Detached
Numb
Withdrawn

UNEASY
Restless
Startled
Surprised
Uncomfortable
Agitated
Troubled
Alarmed
Rattled
Upset
Shocked

EMBARRASSED
Self-conscious
Flustered
Ashamed
Guilty

FATIGUED
Tired
Sleepy
Depleted
Exhausted
Burnt out

PAIN
Hurt
Lonely
Miserable
Regretful
Remorseful
Grief
Heartbroken
Agony

SAD
Unhappy
Heavyhearted
Disappointed
Discouraged
Hopeless
Dejected
Despair

TENSE
Anxious
Cranky
Distressed
Irritable
Nervous
Overwhelmed
Stressed out

VULNERABLE
Fragile
Sensitive
Guarded
Reserved
Insecure
Helpless

YEARNING
Wistful
Longing
Envious
Jealous

LIST OF NEEDS

Note: Parents and children often express relatively few needs most of the time, and longer lists available online become overwhelming to use. Try starting with this shorter list and look for more precise words once you get the hang of it.

CONNECTION
Acceptance
Appreciation
Belonging
Collaboration
Communication
Empathy
Kindness
Love
Partnership
Support
To understand and
 be understood
Touch
Trust

PEACE
Beauty
Calm
Ease
Harmony
Order
Respect

HONESTY
Authenticity
Integrity
Presence

MEANING
Challenge
Competence
 (especially in
 parenting)
Creativity
Growth
Having a sense
 of purpose
Hope
Learning
Self-connection
Self-expression

SAFETY
Consistency
Physical and
 emotional safety

AUTONOMY
Choice
Freedom
Independence
Power
Space/freedom
 from touch

**RELAXATION/
LEISURE**
Excitement
Fun
Humor
Indulgence
Joy
Mental space
Play
Pleasure

**PHYSICAL
WELL-BEING**
Air
Comfort
Exercise
Food/water
Rest/sleep
Safety
Safety of children/
 dependents
Self-care
Sexual expression

STARTER SCRIPTS

Use these starter scripts to help you work through a Problem-Solving Conversation with your child:

> "I've noticed we're having a hard time . . ."
> "It seems like we're struggling when . . ."
> "Would it be OK if we talk about that?"

> "Could you tell me how you were feeling when that happened?"
> "What was going on for you when that happened?"
> "Could you tell me how you feel about . . . ?"
> "I'm wondering if you're feeling . . . ?"
> "I'm feeling . . . right now."

> "What were you trying to do when . . . ?"
> "Can you share why . . . wasn't working for you?"
> "Can you tell me why you don't want to . . . ?"
> "I'm trying to . . ."
> "I have a need for . . ."

> "Would you be willing to . . . ?"
> "If I were to . . . , would that help?"
> "Do you think we could try . . . ?"

FEELINGS CUPCAKES

Make a copy of this page (or download a full-size one from https://
www.YourParentingMojo.com/BookBonuses), then refer to the feelings lists on page 206 and fill in your cherry and frosting feelings.

YOUR CUPCAKE

Cherry: most common feelings when needs
aren't met ....

....

....

Frosting: next most common feelings when
needs aren't met ....

....

....

Cupcake: consider other feelings

YOUR CHILD'S
CUPCAKE

Cherry: most common feelings when needs
aren't met ....

....

....

Frosting: next most common feelings when
needs aren't met ....

....

....

Cupcake: consider other feelings

NEEDS CUPCAKES

Make a copy of this page (or download a full-size one from https://www.YourParentingMojo.com/BookBonuses), then refer to the needs list on page 208 and fill in your cherry and frosting needs.

YOUR CUPCAKE

Cherry: most common needs

....

....

....

Frosting: next most common needs

....

....

....

Cupcake: consider other needs

YOUR CHILD'S CUPCAKE

Cherry: most common needs

....

....

....

Frosting: next most common needs

....

....

....

Cupcake: consider other needs

NOTES

PREFACE

xi   **"Because everyone around me was White."** *Merriam-Webster*, s.v. "White supremacy," accessed November 26, 2022, https://www.merriam-webster.com/dictionary/white%20supremacy.

xi   **"England's colonial history."** In England, the narrative around the Potato Famine in Ireland was that the potato crop failed due to a fungal infection, so many Irish people emigrated to the United States. I didn't learn until I visited Ireland as an adult that what Irish people call the Great Hunger was largely caused by the mass export of what food was available other than potatoes, which was sent to England to pay rent.
    Sam Porter, "Confronting Famine: The Case of the Irish Great Hunger," *Nursing Inquiry* 5, no. 2 (June 1998): 112–117, https://doi.org/10.1046/j.1440-1800.1998.520112.x.

xii   **"The country's role in the slave trade."** While scholars debate the *extent* to which the slave trade impacted British industrialization, they seem somewhat united in agreeing that it did have an impact. Acemoglu et al. argue that the profits generated by the slave trade allowed the bourgeoisie to enact property rights reforms, which enabled them to trade and invest more.
    Daron Acemoglu, Simon Johnson, and James Robinson, "The Rise of Europe: Atlantic Trade, Institutional Change and Economic Growth," NBER Working Paper Series #9378 (Cambridge, MA: National Bureau of Economic Research, 2002), https://www.nber.org/system/files/working_papers/w9378/w9378.pdf.
    Eltis and Engerman say that the impact was far more limited.
    David Eltis and Stanley L. Engerman, "The Importance of Slavery and the Slave Trade to Industrializing Britain," *The Journal of Economic History* 60, no. 1 (2000): 124–144, https://www.researchgate.net/profile/David-Eltis/publication/23565372_The_Importance_of_Slavery_and_the_Slave_Trade_to_Industrializing_Britain/

links/588e2abb92851cef1362c973/The-Importance-of-Slavery-and
-the-Slave-Trade-to-Industrializing-Britain.pdf).

Thomas Clarkson, a major slave trade abolitionist, was born in
Wisbech (the closest town to where I grew up), a fact that nobody in
school ever thought relevant to discuss.

Encyclopedia Britannica Online, s.v. "Thomas Clarkson,"
accessed March 2022, https://www.britannica.com/biography/
Thomas-Clarkson.

xii   **"Cultures of recent immigrants."** Labor shortages after World
War II led the British government to encourage immigration from
Commonwealth countries (especially India, Pakistan, and the
Caribbean), primarily in low-skilled roles in manufacturing for lower
pay than White workers. White British people perceived their way
of life to be superior to that of immigrants from the former colonies,
who were often construed as "'backward,' 'untrustworthy,' with crim-
inal tendencies, hyper-sexualized, and prone to over-breeding."

Farzana Shain, "Race, Nation, and Education: An Overview of
British Attempts to 'Manage Diversity' Since the 1950s," *Education
Inquiry* 4, no. 1 (2013): 63–85, https://doi.org/10.3402/edui.v4i1.22062.

xiii   **"Fear of open conflict, and individualism."** Tema Okun's paper
describing the characteristics I mention, as well as several others
that are more relevant in business contexts for which Okun originally
developed these ideas, can be found at:

Tema Okun, "White Supremacy Culture," accessed
November 5, 2022, https://www.whitesupremacyculture.info/
uploads/4/3/5/7/43579015/okun_-_white_sup_culture_2020.pdf.

xiv   **"While interviewing an expert on intergenerational trauma for
my podcast."** There isn't always a one-to-one correlation between
the difficult experiences we've had as children and how these show
up in our lives as adults, and everyone copes with their experiences differently. See: "Reducing the Impact of Intergenerational
Trauma," July 22, 2018, https://www.yourparentingmojo.com/
IntergenerationalTrauma.

xiv   **"Contents of my innards to explode out."** I've known for a couple of years now that my body's major "tell" that something isn't right is a crippling knot deep in my intestines. Sometimes I describe it as "nausea," although there's never any danger I'll throw up because it's further down than that. It was only in writing this sentence for this book that I realized my body has been sending me this signal for decades. Now I can look back on times when I was going home in my teenage years and experienced the same sensation. No matter how long or how well we stuff it down, *our bodies know what's happening.*

xv   **"A first-time homeowner's loan."** While outright denials of housing are less common now than in the past, Black applicants are 60 percent more likely to be denied a home loan even when income, gender, and credit worthiness are statistically controlled.

Lincoln Quillian, John J. Lee, and Brandon Honoré, "Racial Discrimination in the U.S. Housing and Mortgage Lending Markets: A Quantitative Review of Trends," *Race and Social Problems*, 12, no. 1 (2020); 13–28.

AUTHOR'S NOTE

xxii   **"Forced separations of Indigenous families."** The separation of Indigenous families is often a mediator for current substance use (which is seen as an individual's problem).

Melissa D. Zephier Olson and Kirk Dombrowski, "A Systematic Review of Indian Boarding Schools and Attachment in the Context of Substance Use Studies of Native Americans," *Journal of Racial and Ethnic Health Disparities* 7, no. 1 (2019): 62–71.

xxii   **"Government-sanctioned breakups of families through the mechanism of slavery."** Angela Davis, "Reflections on the Black Woman's Role in the Community of Slaves," *The Massachusetts Review* 13, no. 1/2 (1972): 81–100.

xxii **"Overrepresentation of Indigenous and Black children in foster care."** Child Welfare Information Gateway, US Department of Health and Human Services, Administration for Children and Families, Children's Bureau, "Child Welfare Practice to Address Racial Disproportionality and Disparity," (2021), https://www.childwelfare.gov/pubpdfs/racial_disproportionality.pdf.

xxii **"Closing 'gaps' between the success of Indigenous/Black children and White children."** Nancy Kober, "It Takes More Than Testing: Closing the Achievement Gap. A Report of the Center on Education Policy," Accessed February 7, 2023, https://files.eric.ed.gov/fulltext/ED454358.pdf.

xxii **"Using interventions like grit and a growth mindset."** I discuss the research on grit in the episode: "Grit: The Unique Factor in Your Child's Success?" December 3, 2017, https://www.yourparentingmojo.com/Grit.

I discuss the research on growth mindset in the episode: "Can Growth Mindset Live Up To The Hype?" April 9, 2018, https://www.yourparentingmojo.com/GrowthMindset.

xxii **"Assumes all parents want the same things for their child as a privileged White person does."** For a compelling discussion on what one Black parent wants for her daughter and their family unit, see: Dani McClain, *We Live for the We* (New York: Bold Type, 2019).

xxvii **"Genitalia are ambiguous more often than we might think."** Thyen et al. found an ambiguous genitalia prevalence rate of two per ten thousand live births in Germany.

Ute Thyen, Kathrin Lanz, Paul-Martin Holterhaus, and Olaf Hiort, "Epidemiology and Initial Management of Ambiguous Genitalia at Birth in Germany," *Hormone Research* 66 (2006): 195–203.

xxvii **"Antiracist policies."** See "Your Parenting Mojo's Anti-Racist Policies" at https://yourparentingmojo.com/anti-racism/.

"BIPOC (Black, Indigenous, and People of Color)." I know this term isn't preferred by everyone and may especially not resonate for people located outside the United States. Given that the book is being written in the US about challenges that were often created in the US and other Eurocentric cultures and exported with colonialism, and for a primarily US-based audience, and because BIPOC is currently the preferred term that does not center Whiteness (as "non-White" does), I will use it while acknowledging its imperfections.

Constance Grady, "Why the Term 'BIPOC' Is So Complicated, Explained by Linguists," Vox, June 30, 2020, https://www.vox.com/2020/6/30/21300294/bipoc-what-does-it-mean-critical-race-linguistics-jonathan-rosa-deandra-miles-hercules.

CHAPTER 1: SOCIETAL FORCES SHAPE OUR FAMILY LIFE

12 **"Whiteness holds value has been exported along with colonization and now permeates many cultures."** Ibram X. Kendi outlines the ways that different groups of immigrants, as well as African Americans, look down on each other: "That is the central double standard in ethnic racism: loving one's position on the ladder above other ethnic groups and hating one's position below that of other ethnic groups."

Ibram X. Kendi, *How to Be an Antiracist* (New York: One World, 2019), 66.

12 **"Express *their* full humanity."** For more information on this topic (written in very accessible language), see:

Tema Okun, "What Is White Supremacy Culture?" White Supremacy Culture, May 23, 2022, https://www.whitesupremacyculture.info/what-is-it.html.

14 **"Whiteness is seen as the default and best way of existing."** There's a compelling collection of views on mothering by "radical mothers of color" in:

Alexis Pauline Gumbs, China Martens, Mai'a Williams, and Loretta J. Ross, *Revolutionary Mothering: Love on the Front Lines* (Toronto: Between the Lines, and Oakland: PM Press, 2016).

See especially Alexis Pauline Gumbs's essay, "Forget Hallmark: Why Mother's Day Is a Queer Black Left Feminist Thing," page 117.

14 **"Remove the stressors of poverty and racism."** See, for example, how research on middle class White children conducted in the 1930s shows up in the *Your X-Year-Old Child* books published in the 1980s that are still recommended in parenting groups today. "Why We Shouldn't Discuss the Your X-Year-Old Child Books Anymore," December 4, 2022, https://yourparentingmojo.com/YourXYearOldChild/.

15 **"Brian Stout."** Brian runs the Building Belonging community at https://www.buildingbelonging.us/.

15 **"Dr. Carol Gilligan."** Brian Stout and I interviewed Dr. Gilligan about how patriarchy impacts parenting in the episode "Patriarchy is Perpetuated Through Parenting (Part 1)," February 23, 2020, https://yourparentingmojo.com/Patriarchy.

15 **"Naomi Snider."** Carol Gilligan and Naomi Snider, *Why Does Patriarchy Persist?* (Cambridge, UK: Polity, 2018).
I should acknowledge that Dr. Gilligan's work has been criticized by feminist researchers for allowing the voices of primarily privileged White girls and women to stand for the voices of all girls and women, ignoring the effects of race, class, sexuality, and ability. For more on this topic, see especially Chapter 2 in:
Sinikka Aapola, Marnina Gonick, and Anita Harris, *Young Femininity: Girlhood, Power, and Social Change* (Basingstoke: Palgrave Macmillan, 2005).

16 **"Male domination has not destroyed."** bell hooks, *Talking Back: Thinking Feminist, Thinking Black* (Boston: South End Press, 1989), 131.

17 **"Mothers feeling a deep sense of anger."** See the personal essay:
Masana Ndinga-Kanga, "The Necessity of Rage and the Politics of Feminist Parenting," in *Feminist Parenting: Perspectives from Africa and Beyond*, ed. Rama Salla Dieng and Andrea O'Reilly, (Bradford: Demeter, 2020), 163–176.

18   **"This has to begin on the level of the family."** bell hooks, "bell hooks on the Roots of Male Violence Against Women," interview by Rhiannon Corby and David Remnick, *The New Yorker Radio Hour*, WNYC, November 16, 2017, Retrieved from https://www.wnycstudios.org/podcasts/tnyradiohour/segments/ bell-hooks-roots-male-violence-against-women.

18   **"Theologian Brian McLaren contradicts this view."** Quoted in Jess Rimington & Joanna L. Cea, *Beloved Economies: Transforming How We Work*, (Vancouver, B.C.: Page Two, 2022).

18   **"Returning a small portion of the excess in charitable good deeds."** For a compelling exploration of how the super-rich impact policy through their 'charitable' giving, see: Anand Giridharadas, *Winners Take All: The Elite Charade of Changing the World*, (New York, NY: Knopf, 2018).

18   **"Historian Dr. Heather Cox Richardson observes."** Heather Cox Richardson, April 7, 2021. Letters from an American. Blog post. Retrieved from: https://heathercoxrichardson.substack.com/p/ april-7-2021.

19   **"Most effective advertising campaigns ever."** The diamond cartel De Beers created the one-month salary "rule," which blossomed over time to two and then three months.
        Laurence Cawley, "De Beers Myth: Do People Spend a Month's Salary on a Diamond Engagement Ring?" *BBC News Magazine*, May 16, 2014, https://www.bbc.com/news/magazine-27371208.

20   **"Using BIPOC people's labor."** See, for example: Matthieu Aikins, "How is Your Phone Powered? Problematically." *New York Times*, January 23, 2023, https://www.nytimes.com/2023/01/23/books/ review/cobalt-red-siddharth-kara.html.

20   **"Waste products dumped in the water/land/air closest to where BIPOC people live."** See, for example: Paul Mohai and Robin Saha, "Which Came First, People or Pollution? A Review of Theory and Evidence Form Longitudinal Environmental Justice Studies," *Environmental Research Letters*, December 22, 2015, https://iopscience. iop.org/article/10.1088/1748-9326/10/12/125011/pdf.

20 **"People in Eurocentric countries are responsible for most of the greenhouse gas emissions."** Different accounting mechanisms apportion responsibility in different ways; one newer approach uses countries' actual emissions from 1850 to 1969, and consumption-based emissions from 1970 to 2015, since it doesn't seem fair that China be held responsible for emissions associated with Eurocentric countries' consumption.

Jason Hickel, "Quantifying National Responsibility for Climate Breakdown: An Equality-Based Attribution Approach for Carbon Dioxide Emissions in Excess of the Planetary Boundary" *The Lancet Planetary Health*, September 2020, https://www.thelancet.com/journals/lanplh/article/PIIS2542-5196(20)30196-0/fulltext.

20 **"Which primarily affects BIPOC people."** See: "Climate Change and Land: An IPCC Special Report on Climate Change, Deforestation, Land Degradation, Sustainable Land Management, Food Security, and Greenhouse Gas Fluxes in Terrestrial Ecosystems," The Intergovernmental Panel on Climate Change, 2022, Accessed February 8, 2023, https://www.ipcc.ch/srccl/download/.

20 **"Black women have not found freedom from sexism."** bell hooks, *Ain't I a Woman: Black Women and Feminism*, New Edition (New York: Routledge, 2015).

20 **"Money has provided the illusion of security."** These ideas (and more) are expanded more fully in Charles Eisenstein's great book *Sacred Economics*, which J. D. recommended to me. *Sacred Economics* is available in bookstores, and on a gift-economy basis at https://charleseisenstein.org/books/sacred-economics/. I downloaded and read the book for free, and then donated more than the cover price via his website. Charles also graciously provided insights into how to publish a book on a gift-economy basis, which I used when writing this book.

21 **"White women are punished."** Pragya Agarwal, "Not Very Likable: Here Is How Bias Is Affecting Women Leaders," *Forbes*, October 23, 2018, https://www.forbes.com/sites/pragyaagarwaleurope/2018/10/23/not-very-likable-here-is-how-bias-is-affecting-women-leaders.

21   **"Black women are punished."** Michele Wallace, *Black Macho and the Myth of the Superwoman* (Miamisburg, OH: Verso, 2015).

26   **"In a podcast interview, parent Amy."** See: "Reparenting Ourselves to Create Empathy in the World with Amy," January 23, 2022, https://www.yourparentingmojo.com/Amy.

32   **"Patriarchy is killing them about as much as it's killing White women."** See, for example:
       Matthew Jakupcak, "Masculine Gender Role Stress and Men's Fear of Emotions as Predictors of Self-Reported Aggression and Violence," *Violence and Victims* 18, no. 5 (2003): 433–541.
       Louise Lynch, Maggie Long, and Anne Moorehead, "Young Men, Help-Seeking, and Mental Health Services: Exploring Barriers and Solution," *American Journal of Men's Health* 12, no. 1 (2016): 138–149.
       G. Barker, C. Ricardo, M. Nascimento, A. Olukoya, and C. Santos, "Questioning Gender Norms with Men to Improve Health Outcomes: Evidence of Impact," *Global Public Health* 5, no. 5 (2010): 539–553.
       Kristina Orth-Gomer, Annika Rosengren, and Lars Wilhelmsen, "Lack of Social Support and Incidence of Coronary Heart Disease in Middle-Aged Swedish Men," *Psychosomatic Medicine* 55, no. 1 (1993): 37–43.
       All of these studies and more are described and analyzed in:
       Liz Plank, *For the Love of Men: From Toxic to a More Mindful Masculinity* (New York: St. Martin's, 2019).

33   **"The kinds of relationships Indigenous parents used to have."** Andrea Landry, "How I'm Raising My Daughter to be 100 Percent, Unapologetically Indigenous," *Today's Parent*, May 22, 2021, https://www.todaysparent.com/family/parenting/how-im-raising-my-daughter-to-be-100-percent-unapologetically-indigenous/.

33   **"Before White people tried to kill and then assimilate them."** Information on this specific fact sourced from:
       Becky Little, "How Boarding Schools Tried to 'Kill the Indian' through Assimilation," History.com, (November 1, 2018), https://www.history.com/news/how-boarding-schools-tried-to-kill-the-indian-through-assimilation.

I invite you to check who the local tribe(s) are in your area at https://native-land.ca/, and then learn about their specific history and practices, and talk with your children about them. To counteract the stereotypical "Native people were the first inhabitants but they aren't here anymore" stereotype, you could pair this with a reading of:

Adrienne Keene, *Notable Native People: 50 Indigenous Leaders, Dreamers, and Changemakers from Past and Present* (New York: Penguin Random House, 2021).

We read a page every evening over dinner, and before that, we read the Black History Flashcards (featuring many people who are still alive) available from https://www.urbanintellectuals.com.

CHAPTER 2: JUDGMENTS, REWARDS, AND PUNISHMENTS

41 **"Judging is how we compare people's performance."** "Masculinity as Homophobia: Fear, Shame, and Silence in the Construction of Gender Identity," in *Feminism and Masculinities*, ed. Peter F. Murphy (Oxford: Oxford University Press, 2004), 182–199.

43 **"Judgments, rewards, and punishments do 'work' to change a child's behavior."** The research on this topic is discussed in the podcast episode "Should We Go Ahead and Heap Rewards on our Kid?" October 14, 2018, https://yourparentingmojo.com/captivate-podcast/Rewards/.

44 **"Eating their vegetables."** The research on this topic is dicussed in the episode "Help, My Toddler Won't Eat Their Vegetables," October 10, 2016, https://yourparentingmojo.com/captivate-podcast/007-help-toddler-wont-eat-vegetables/.

44 **"Sharing with a sibling."** In an admittedly tiny study of twenty-one children, children whose mothers did not reward the child after observing prosocial behavior or engage in "empathy training" after observing its absence were the most likely to exhibit that behavior again, although the effect was small. But proponents of rewards

would expect the opposite result: rewarding behavior should lead to increased frequency of use.

Joan E. Grusec, "Socializing Concern for Others in the Home," *Developmental Psychology* 27, no. 2 (1991): 338–342.

44 **"Once we cut off the rewards."** Dr. Alan Kazdin has been researching contingent rewards for decades, and concluded back in 1982 that "token economy" schemes can be effective at changing behavior in the short term, but that there's always a danger of client resistance to the program as well as backsliding. Surprisingly, his Kazdin Method for Parenting claims to be able to "improve your effectiveness in changing your child's behavior . . . without throwing rewards at your child." But his book describing this method contains three pages of suggested rewards in the appendix.

Alan Kazdin, *The Kazdin Method for Parenting the Defiant Child* (New York: Harper Paperbacks, 2009).

45 **"The fear of being spanked again."** For an in-depth review of the research on spanking, see the episode "Is Spanking a Child Really So Bad?" February 6, 2022, https://www.yourparentingmojo.com/Spanking.

45 **"Brené Brown."** Brené Brown, "So many of us are better at inflicting pain than healing it. We push hurt onto others," Facebook, October 2, 2015, https://www.facebook.com/brenebrown/photos/d41d8cd9/1159176027430838/.

47 **"Another parent, Cassie, rewarded her children."** Cassie and her partner started using rewards on their pediatrician's advice. Perhaps it might surprise you to learn that pediatricians are trained to diagnose and treat illness and disease, but not to support children's development? Most pediatricians are most concerned with reducing the greatest harm, which I believe is why the handouts I received at toddler checkups advised using time-outs instead of spanking.

53 **"Rescuers were more likely to have been raised to behave in ways that were aligned with their values."** Mark Klempner, *The Heart Has Reasons: Holocaust Rescuers and Their Stories of Courage* (Cleveland: The Pilgrim Press, 2006).

54   **"Shift our language."** There's a fascinating line of research in linguistics that looks at how the language we use shapes our experience. Students asked about a filmed car accident where one car "smashed" another estimated that the car was going significantly faster than students who were asked how fast the cars were going when they "contacted" each other.

Elizabeth F. Loftus and John C. Palmer, "Reconstruction of Automobile Destruction: An Example of the Interaction Between Language and Memory," *Journal of Verbal Learning and Verbal Behavior* 13, no. 5 (1974): 585–589.

College students who unscrambled sentences related to economic language show less compassion toward others when delivering bad news.

Andrew L. Molinsky, Adam M. Grant, and Joshua D. Margolis, "The Bedside Manner of Homo Economicus: How and Why Priming an Economic Schema Reduces Compassion," *Organizational Behavior and Human Decision Processes* 119 (2012): 27–37.

And students who are primed to think of themselves as "consumers" rather than "citizens" feel less responsible for their role in a theoretical water shortage, had lower trust in other parties involved, and were less likely to view the other parties as partners in facing the dilemma.

Monika A. Bauer, James E. B. Wilkie, Jung K. Kim, and Galen V. Bodenhausen, "Cuing Consumerism: Situational Materialism Undermines Personal and Social Well-Being," *Psychological Science* 23, no. 5 (2012): 517–523.

Language thus shapes how we show up in our families and in the wider world, so making the decision to change this changes our experience and how we interact with others.

56   **"Endorsed by sleep specialist Dr. Chris Winter."** My interview on this topic can be found at: "The Rested Child with Dr. Chris Winter," October 17, 2021, https://yourparentingmojo.com/RestedChild/.

I also coach two parents on how to apply this approach in the episode "No Set Bedtime with Gila and Katherine," January 30, 2022, at https://www.yourparentingmojo.com/NoSetBedtime.

58   **"Convey messages about our status."** I do acknowledge that
      BIPOC parents want to make sure their children appear well kept so
      that White parents and teachers don't call Child Protective Services,
      and the onus is on White parents and teachers to look for real evi-
      dence of harm before making this call.

CHAPTER 3: EMOTIONS AND REGULATION

62   **"Zero to Three published the results of a parent survey."** The
      results of this study are discussed in the press release: "Parent Survey
      Reveals Expectation Gap for Parents of Young Children," Zero to
      Three, October 13, 2016, Retrieved from: https://www.zerotothree.
      org/resource/parent-survey-reveals-expectation-gap-for-parents-of-
      young-children/. The full report to which the press release refers is no
      longer available on the organization's website.

68   **"The four defining attributes of empathy."** Theresa Wiseman,
      "A Concept Analysis of Empathy," *Journal of Advanced Nursing* 23
      (1996): 1162–1167, https://www.researchgate.net/profile/Theresa-
      Wiseman/publication/227941757_A_concept_analysis_of_empathy/
      links/5b9a33774585153105844028/A-concept-analysis-of-empathy.pdf.

69   **"Our way of understanding the world."** For example, police officers
      who were investigating Black British teenager Stephen Lawrence's
      murder after a racially motivated attack perceived his family's mourn-
      ing as a lack of cooperation with their investigation.
          Simon Holdaway and Megan O'Neill, "Institutional Racism after
      Macpherson: An Analysis of Police Views," *Policing & Society* 16, no. 4
      (2006): 349–369.

73   **"Consider other possibilities."** There's a sample List of Feelings
      on pages 206 and 207 that's shorter than many other lists available
      online and that is also organized by intensity of feeling, which you
      may find makes it easier to use.

75   **"Dr. Jacquelyn Fede made a dinosaur energy-meter."** Dr. Fede
describes the energy meter in an interview on the *Autism Journeys*
podcast episode "Interview With Austim Level Up, Autism Journeys
2020," https://open.spotify.com/episode/7csA8BmFEcIj9aoRYfzwJp.

CHAPTER 4: CHILDREN'S RESISTANCE

80   **"Drawn from Non-Violent Communication."** I want to acknowledge that Marshall Rosenberg's work on nonviolent communication
has been criticized by some because it can embed rather than contribute to breaking down traditional power structures. It's absolutely
possible for a person with more power to require another person to
stick closely to the process, not recognize their feelings and needs as
valid because they aren't expressed in the "correct" way, listen with the
intent of one-upping rather than empathy and compassion, and appear
to be taking the other person's needs into account without actually
doing this. I don't claim to address all of these critiques, but within the
context of a parent-child relationship, I believe that where the parent is
listening with a genuine attempt to understand and hold both their and
their child's needs with equal care that we are moving toward a world
where children are genuinely respected. For more on this, see:

Ray Taylor, "Helpful critique of NVC," Facebook, August 17, 2011,
https://www.facebook.com/notes/nvca-for-empathy-requests-support
/helpful-critique-of-nvc/217963308252441/.

Raffi Marhaba, "Nonviolent Communication Is For the Privileged,"
Collectively Free, May 2, 2022, https://www.collectivelyfree.org
/nonviolent-communication-privileged/.

Meenadchi, *Decolonizing Non-Violent Communication* (Los Angeles:
Co-Conspirator, 2018).

80   **"Marshall Rosenberg."** Marshall B. Rosenberg, *Nonviolent
Communication: A Language of Compassion.* (Encinitas, CA:
Puddledancer, 1999).

Inbal Kashtan was a pioneer in using NVC principles with children;
her book is short and very useful:

Inbal Kashtan, *Parenting From Your Heart: Sharing the Gifts of
Compassion, Connection, and Choice* (Encinitas, CA: Puddledancer, 2005).

82 **"Misattribute their motives."** Dr. Chris Niebauer reviews the evidence for this misattribution in his really interesting book *No Self, No Problem* (I interviewed him about it in the episode "No Self, No Problem," May 24, 2020, https://www.yourparentingmojo.com/Self). My favorite is the study where men walked across either a high, wobbly suspension bridge or a low, solid concrete bridge, and then were offered an attractive research assistant's phone number so they could 'ask questions about the study' if they wanted to. Heterosexual men who crossed the suspension bridge were significantly more likely to misinterpret their fear as arousal, and call the research assistant.

D. G. Dutton and A. P. Aaron, "Some Evidence For Heightened Sexual Attraction Under Conditions of High Anxiety," *Journal of Personality and Social Psychology* 30(4) (1974): 510–517.

Once we've misattributed, our left brains (which is where language processing happens) makes up an explanation for what happened that fits with our prior experiences which may have no basis in reality.

Michael S. Gazzaniga, "The Split Brain Revisited," *Scientific American* 279(1), (July 1998): 50–55.

These studies are cited in: Chris Niebauer, *No Self, No Problem: How Neuropsychology Is Catching Up to Buddhism* (San Antonio: Hierophant, 2019).

83 **"To make sense of my experiences that are only tangentially connected to reality."** I also explored the lack of connection between our thoughts and reality in my conversation with Dr. Neibauer. In our culture we perceive that our thoughts are the truth, so the idea that we don't actually have to believe them can be revelatory and enormously freeing. Learn more at https://www.yourparentingmojo.com/Self and in his book *No Self, No Problem*.

84 **"The National Sleep Foundation recommends."** I was amused to dig into the methodology section of this paper, which basically involved asking a lot of sleep doctors "How much sleep do you think children should get?" and determining the number of hours endorsed by the majority of the doctors.

Max Hirshkowitz, Kaitlyn Whiton, Steven M. Albert, et al., "National Sleep Foundation's Sleep Time Durations: Methodology and Results Summary," *Sleep Health* 1, no. 1 (2015): 40–43.

90   **"adrienne maree brown."** adrienne maree brown, *Pleasure Activism: The Politics of Feeling Good* (Chico, CA: AK Press, 2019).

90   **"Dr. Miki Kashtan."** Miki Kashtan, *Spinning Threads of Radical Aliveness: Transcending the Legacy of Separation in Our Individual Lives* (Oakland: Fearless Heart, 2014).

CHAPTER 5: MEETING PARENTS' NEEDS

96   **"Dr. Alice Miller tells a story."** The "giftedness" described in her book isn't in the academic sense but in the sense of being able to navigate difficult family dynamics.
       Alice Miller, *The Drama of the Gifted Child: The Search for True Self* (New York: Basic, 1997).

97   **"Podcast episode discussing the parental burnout."** See the episode "Parental Burn Out," April 26, 2020, https://www. yourparentingmojo.com/Burnout.

98   **"René Descartes."** There is some disagreement about whether Descartes actually held the ideas that we now name the "Cartesian split," but whatever its origin, the concept is alive and well in White-supremacy-based cultures.
       Lilli Alanen, "Descartes's Dualism and the Philosophy of Mind," *Revue de metaphysique et de morale* 94, no. 3 (1989): 391–413.

102   **"Regularly occurring needs."** We should avoid trying to think of one need as more important than another. We may have read about Maslow's hierarchy of needs, but the hierarchy was an idea superimposed on Maslow's work by management consultants!
       Todd Bridgman, Stephen Cummings, and John A. Ballard, "Who Built Maslow's Pyramid? A History of the Creation of Management Studies' Most Famous Symbol and its Implications for Management Education," *Academy of Management Learning & Education* 18, no. 1 (2019): 81–98.
       The popular view of Maslow's work is that self-actualization is a need that comes much later in life and only once earlier needs like

physiological and belongingness needs are met. I'm reminded of a parent I work with whose preschooler exerts a great deal of control over what she eats, and if a parent comments on what the child is eating, the child refuses to eat. This child has such a need for autonomy that she's willing to override her need for food to meet it. Another parent recalls that her father would yell at and hit her regularly, and one time told her to stay in her room without food or bathroom access (except when her brother acted as lookout) until she apologized for talking back to him. For an entire week, she put her need for dignity and authenticity in her relationship with her father above her need for basic sustenance, and the point at which she was forced to deny these needs marked a turning point in her relationship with her father. She went on to develop an eating disorder that she believes has its roots in her effort to not "cave in" via the guilt related to being inauthentic to herself so she could get access to food. Now anytime she feels she needs to stand up for herself, she experiences an intense fear that some form of nourishment will be taken away. Clearly, "basic" needs like food do not always take precedence over "higher-order" needs like autonomy.

102 **"*The Shameless Mom Academy* podcast."** Sara Dean, "Jen Lumanlan: Taming Your Triggers in Motherhood," February 9, 2022, in *The Shameless Mom Academy*, podcast, https://shamelessmom.com/episode/jen-lumanlan-taming-your-triggers-in-motherhood/.

102 **"The *FamilyPreneur* podcast."** Meg Brunson, "Taming Your Triggers with Jen Lumanlan," February 2, 2022, in *FamilyPreneur*, podcast, https://www.youtube.com/watch?v=Wd7Qi8dd3Sk.

110 **"Respect our child's boundaries whenever we can."** I know some parents take this to its logical conclusion and respect *all* of a child's boundaries. If a child says they don't want to have a vaccination or medication or a medical procedure recommended by a doctor, the parent will respect the child's boundaries. I personally believe it's necessary to balance respect for our child's boundaries with knowledge of their brain development, which will prioritize avoiding the momentary discomfort of an injection over a life-preserving medical procedure. There may still be ways to meet the child's needs even within these scenarios.

CHAPTER 6: PROBLEM-SOLVING CONVERSATIONS

136 **"Adrianna and Tim."** See the episode: "From Desperation to Collaboration with Adrianna & Tim," May 15, 2022, https://yourparentingmojo.com/Desperation/.

CHAPTER 7: COMMON DIFFICULTIES WITH PROBLEM-SOLVING CONVERSATIONS

138 **"Largely geared toward the adults' perspective."** Miki Kashtan, *Spinning Threads of Radical Aliveness* (Oakland, CA: Fearless Heart, 2014), 45.

139 **"Their behavior causes us to revisit that old trauma of rejection by our parents."** My conversation with Dr. van der Kolk is in the episode: "The Body Keeps The Score," July 25, 2021, https://yourparentingmojo.com/TheBodyKeepsTheScore.

141 **"Plan to practice self-compassion."** I recorded an interview with Dr. Susan Pollak looking at the research and practices on this topic in the episode: "Self-Compassion for Parents," October 18, 2020, https://www.yourparentingmojo.com/SelfCompassion.

143 **"Choice point."** Learn how to use tools from acceptance and commitment therapy in my interview with Dr. Diana Hill: "Psychological Flexibility through ACT with Dr. Diana Hill," May 23, 2021, https://yourparentingmojo.com/ACT.

144 **"When we make amends by retelling the story."** I explored this approach in the episode "How Family Storytelling Can Help You To Develop Closer Relationships And Overcome Struggles," May 7, 2018 https://yourparentingmojo.com/FamilyStorytelling.

154 **"Parent Jamie navigates both ADHD."** Jamie doesn't find diagnoses to be particularly helpful but finds that ADHD describes a particular constellation of differences and challenges she faces.

CHAPTER 8: LEVELING UP

168 **"American Academy of Pediatrics' (AAP) current guidelines on screen time."** The full guidelines are explained at:

American Academy of Pediatrics, "Where We Stand: Screen Time," Accessed February 7, 2023, https://www.healthychildren.org/English/family-life/Media/Pages/Where-We-Stand-TV-Viewing-Time.aspx.

I produced a podcast episode after the guidelines changed to understand why the updates were made: https://yourparentingmojo.com/Screen-Time.

I also interviewed a former President of the AAP and explored how these guidelines are created in the episode "Ask the American Academy of Pediatrics!" July 21, 2019, https://yourparentingmojo.com/AAP.

170 **"I've produced a number of podcast episodes on this topic."** See my conversation with Dr. Michael Goran (whose book seems to have somewhat overstated the research on the potential of sugar to cause harm) in the episode "How to Sugarproof Your Kids with Dr. Michael Goran," October 3, 2021, https://yourparentingmojo.com/captivate-podcast/SugarProof, and "Sugar Rush with Dr. Karen Throsby," January 2, 2022 (looking at the social implications of sugar restrictions), https://yourparentingmojo.com/captivate-podcast/SugarRush. I also coached a parent on how to navigate her child's sugar intake in the episode "Sugar! with Rose Amanda," May 5, 2019, https://yourparentingmojo.com/captivate-podcast/RoseAmanda/.

177 **"How we see chores in Eurocentric cultures."** Before making a pleasant activity (screen time, time with a parent, ice cream) a reward for an unpleasant activity (cleaning up, homework, brushing teeth), consider that research on children's eating indicates that making children eat vegetables to get dessert just makes them like dessert more and vegetables less, and the only behavior that's correlated with the amount of vegetables children eat is . . . how much they like vegetables. See the episode: "Help! My Toddler Won't Eat Vegetables," October 10, 2016, https://yourparentingmojo.com/007-help-toddler-wont-eat-vegetables/.

Rewarding a child for doing "unpleasant" tasks is likely to just make them dislike the task more. Far better to try to make the task pleasant, perhaps by doing it together, or accept the child's help on another task and do this one yourself. See the episode "How do I get my child to do chores?" April 16, 2017, https://yourparentingmojo. com/chores/.

AFTERWORD: WE'RE ALL IN THIS TOGETHER

184 **"Gender nonbinary activist Alok."** See their interview at:
Justin Baldoni, Liz Plank, and Jamey Heath, "ALOK: The Urgent Need for Compassion," July 26, 2021, in *The Man Enough Podcast*, https://www.youtube.com/watch?v=Tq3C9R8HNUQ

184 **"Truly create our village."** See Tami Simon's interview of the Reverend angel Kyodo williams:
Tami Simon, "The Core of Belonging," September 14, 2021, in *Sounds True*, podcast, https://resources.soundstrue.com/podcast/ the-core-of-belonging/.

184 **"Via podcast episodes."** My collection of episodes and blog posts about race can be found at https://www.yourparentingmojo.com/Race.

190 **"Join a reparations group."** There are a number of these available; I'm electing to not provide URLs to protect them from being flooded by potential spam.

190 **"Dean Spade."** Dean Spade, *Mutual Aid: Building Solidarity During This Crisis (and the Next)* (Brooklyn: Verso, 2020). I interviewed Dean about the book in the episode "Healing and Helping with Mutual Aid with Dean Spade," September 25, 2022, https://www.yourparenting- mojo.com/MutualAid.

190　**"Akilah Richards."** See the podcast episode "Doing Self-Directed Education," December 17, 2020, https://yourparentingmojo.com/ FreePeople.

191　**"*Pleasure Activism.*"** adrienne maree brown, *Pleasure Activism: The Politics of Feeling Good* (Oakland, CA: AK Press, 2019).

192　**"Dr. Carol Gilligan and Naomi Snider."** Carol Gilligan and Naomi Snider, *Why Does Patriarchy Persist?* (Cambridge, UK: Polity, 2018).

ACTIONS TO TAKE

205　**"Akilah Richards reminds us."** I interviewed Akilah for a podcast on self-directed education, which she sees as foundational in creating a world where all people are respected. "Doing Self-Directed Education," December 17, 2020, https://yourparentingmojo.com/FreePeople/.

205　**"Nice White Parent."** Chana Joffe-Walt, "Introducing: Nice White Parents," *New York Times*, July 3, 2020, https://www.nytimes. com/2020/07/23/podcasts/nice-white-parents-serial.html.

205　**"Work to reduce the impact of privilege."** Sarah Jaffe's book has some great ideas to start:
　　　Sarah Jaffe, *Wanting What's Best: Parenting, Privilege, and Building a Just World* (Chicago: Parenting Press, 2022).

INDEX